Keeping
the Wood Box Full

Will Ball

Welcome to Wills world 1954 - 1950 - Hope you enjoy the Journey 1-1-2020

i

International Standard Book Number 0-87012-839-6
Library of Congress Control Number 2013921670
Printed in the United States of America
Copyright © 2014 by Will Ball
Greenville, NC
All Rights Reserved
2014

McClain Printing Company
Parsons, WV
www.mcclainprinting.com
2014

TABLE OF CONTENTS

About the Author

Will Ball is a fifth generation descendant of John Annon. John Annon was born in Londenderry, Ireland in 1768. Will grew up on one of the John Annon Farms in Barbour County, West Virginia. He was the seventh son of ten sons lucky enough to be born to the May Annon and Rasty Ball family. He and his nine brothers were also privileged to have a gem of a sister as well.

Will's early career in farming was labor intensive, diverse and provided great training for a do-it-yourselfer. The labor intensive part caught his attention at age six. Around age twelve he announced that he was going to become a hobo and ride the rails. After two to three years of talking about the hobo career May and Rasty became concerned.

After a couple more years, the hobo thought evaporated and Will continued to enjoy school, baseball, basketball, his band and spending time with a favorite girl, Doris M. Wilson.

Will eventually became an Administrator/Educator at East Carolina University (ECU) in Greenville, North Carolina. He taught high school in Ohio and Arizona before locating in Greenville. He retired in 1997 from ECU and every day since then has been Saturday. Even though he enjoyed his career up to the last day of employment, he wanted to enjoy the sunset years. Therefore, he left licenses, certificates, etc. on the wall as well as professional journals and books in the office and closed that chapter of his life.

Will has since begun chronicling these stories about formative years in Barbour County, West Virginia. He lived these stories beginning seventy-nine years ago. They started when May Annon Ball delivered him, gave him a slap on the butt and said, "Welcome, son!" The midwife and Aunt Susie arrived later and were surprised to see that a ten pound plus baby boy had beat them to the event!

Will began writing and performing songs during high school. Some of his most recent songs can be found in the appendices. You will appreciate his love of the mountain state, family heritage and mountain culture imbedded in these stories and songs. You will also understand how the magnetic pull for home has grown stronger and recaptured a native son – the hobo.

Acknowledgements

Thanks to May and Rasty (my mother and father), and all my siblings who taught me about life, the work ethic, keeping promises, do something with your life, how to win people's trust and keep it, how to take my part when needed, and that there were consequences for my behavior.

A special thanks to my wife, Doris, and my children, Micah, Susan, and Donna for listening to and laughing at my stories as I fine-tuned them over and over again. Double thanks to my daughter, Susan, for all the work necessary in deciphering my writing and getting the manuscript to the publisher and especially for her patience in dealing with changes and re-writes.

A big thank you also goes to my sister, Betty, for photographs. Without her 120 Kodak Box Camera, there would not be any candid photos of Rasty's three little shits, my siblings, and May and Rasty. Good job, sis.
I am grateful for other characters in these stories as they enriched my life while living in the great state of West Virginia. Thank you to family and friends for suggesting these stories be chronicled, especially Wendy Post for strongly suggesting, "You'd better do this!" Thanks Wendy.

Introduction: Keeping the Wood Box Full

<u>Keeping the Wood Box Full</u> is about the author's experiences and insights within a family of eleven children during the 1930's, 1940's and 1950's in Barbour County, West Virginia. The stories contained between the covers of this book will provide you with a snail's belly view of what went on in the day to day activities of a family in the Allegheny Mountains during the post-depression years.

Rasty, May, Carl, Betty, Harold, Donald, Lewis, Hayward, Will, Cecil, and David (May's personal farmhands).

Keeping the wood box full was my first permanent chore. I learned early to swing a double hit axe and chop. I chose chopping wood over milking for two reasons. I liked chopping wood and didn't like the milking thing. I wasn't very good at milking, nor did I like getting clobbered by the end of the cow's tail. It always seemed to be full of cockleburs and other nasty stuff. Therefore, I learned to stay ahead of the curve by keeping the wood box full of wood; not just thrown in, but neatly stacked. A neatly stacked wood box not only holds more, but looks better. You know the presentation thing; my sales pitch for keeping that job over milking. I did not, however, get out of having to find the cows and bring them up for milking in the morning.

Why write Keeping the Wood Box Full? After thirty plus years on the Coastal Plains of North Carolina, I began to realize how much I missed the Allegheny Mountains. I also realized I had left richness I could not recapture unless I opened the "memory vault" and wrote about it.

I did not write this to toot my own horn, brag about my up-bringing, or to make me appear special. I believe it is a treatise about all young people raised on small farms in the Allegheny Mountains of West Virginia during the depression years. From my perspective, all of us were in the same boat economically, socially, and morally. Times were tough for most people who lived there. If you wished to be valued, you worked. It wasn't about what you knew, but more about what you could do. Neighbors visited neighbors and helped one another as needed. Older folks visited and sat on the porch to discuss family events, livestock, crops, the weather, religion and how well the President was doing. That part has not changed.

Kids played in the yard, fields, woods, or creek and didn't whine about being "bored". We used our imagination to organize games, build dams, swing on grapevines, build sleds and wagons, not tattle on one another and generally stayed out of trouble. We were wealthy and didn't know it. Thirty plus years later I realized the richness of my childhood and yearned to return to my roots.

Keeping the Wood Box Full is about more than keeping a box full of kindling and firewood. It is about having chores, learning to contribute, fitting in and finding your place in the pecking order of a close knit family. It is also about being nurtured by a mother with a marvelous sense of humor; a mother who managed her work crew (ten sons and a daughter) by example. It is about a mother with boundless energy, laughter and love for her family and friends. Also, it is about a father with a heavy hand, short fuse and who moved methodically in work, deed and thought. He had a hard shell like a turtle, but was mush in the middle. We didn't see much of the mush, his soft side.

Keeping the Wood Box Full contains a box full of stories about growing up in the Allegheny Mountains of West Virginia during the post-depression years. When I think about growing up in a large family, the Moatsville community and Barbour County, memories of people, events, time and places well up in my memory vault. The older I get, the more important these memories become. Our family heritage from the Annon side (Mom's family) began with the birth of John Annon in Londenderry, Ireland. He was born there in 1768. How and when John Annon arrived in America and settled in Barbour County is a puzzle worth unraveling. I hope I can do that one day.

John Annon, his son Zachariah, and Zachariah's son, Henry Annon are my grandfathers. They are buried on the farm where I was born and spent the next eighteen years of my life. My mother, May Annon, was the first child born in our farm house. She was the fourth generation to till the soil on that mountain. Nine brothers, a sister and I were the fifth generation to till the soil there.

The stories in the "Wood Box" are about family, family happenings, relatives, neighbors, and community events that well up from my memory vault. Yes, times were tough, but I believe we were tougher.

I learned most of what I know today from my first eighteen years on the Annon farm.

I cherish that experience and still have a strong attachment to the great state of West Virginia. See "The Place I Call Home" (Appendix).

I have often said that "life was tough and days were long; however, I would not trade my growing up years in Barbour County with anyone I ever met." "Not even the rich of the richest." We were rich and didn't know it. We were rich with freedom to wonder through mountains and streams, rich with strong kinship with family and friends and insulated by our isolation.

I believe my stories are unique to my family; however, other families living in the Alleghenies during 1930-1960 would have their unique stories too. Both sets of stories would be similar in substance, just different characters playing their parts on their stage of life.

Before you dive into Keeping the Wood Box Full, be fore-warned that my writing style is conversational. It may not follow standard rules for tense, verbs, adverbs, adjectives, nouns and so on; you may even occasionally encounter a dangling participle or two. What's a dangling participle? I actually asked a renound English Professor at East Carolina University that question for clarification and immediately regretted that question. I'm better off not knowing about that dangling stuff! I am better off just to write and let words cover the page and ignore form and style. That being said, if my conversational style bothers you, take two readers pills and call me about it in the morning. Continue on if you can handle it.

I now invite you to visit a special time and place with me as I open the "memory vault" and revisit people, events, places, and activities I experienced during the 1930's through the 1950's in Barbour County, West Virginia. And now, as Mom would say, "the dribble is over with so get on with the story".

May and Rasty

My parents, George H. (Rasty) and May Annon Ball.

I woke up this morning thinking about Mom and Dad, May and Rasty Ball, and as I write this it's as if they were sitting across from me at the kitchen table. Their presence in my memory is very sharp and real. They were salt of the earth, real people, well respected in our community, and helped others when needed. They were great parents and kept us under control by keeping us busy with chores and work on a mountain top farm in Barbour County, West Virginia. They provided

1

parental guidance and support for our formative years, as well as the security and love we needed. That love, understood, but not spoken, was the foundation for tight family ties then and still today. I hope most families have that bond. I can't speak for others in the family, but I feel joined at the hip, so to speak, with my parents, brothers and sister. If I needed help, support, money, counsel and a listening ear, they'd fulfill my needs in a heartbeat. They were and are great! I had nine brothers and one sister. Big families were the norm for our time and place in the Alleghenies (1925-1970). About 95 percent of all families lived on small farms (50 to 100 acres) and scratched out most of what they ate from those farms. Another son or daughter added one more hand to the labor pool; everybody worked. We didn't have, "but I don't want to", in our vocabulary. If we did, it was quickly removed by an older brother or most likely one of the parents. In either event, we didn't say "but I don't want to", again. We went with the work crew for the day and worked. In the 1930's, 1940's, 1950's, and 1960's, everyone on those small farms could do something and we learned to work like everyone else.

The parents taught us, showed us, and instilled the work ethic in us every day. We learned early that you were respected for what you could "do" and not as much for what you "knew". The "knew" thing came later.

Mom and Dad, along with other farmers in our corner of Barbour County, were true pioneers. Mom was born on the Annon Farm in 1907. Dad was born in Moatsville in 1899. Adjoining neighbors were about their age, mostly older. Our farm practices were two hundred years old, tried and true, but eons behind the times as far as I

2

was concerned. A team of horses or mules and a few pieces of horse drawn equipment and machinery were all we needed on the farm. Farming during my tenure was labor intensive and just plain tiring. Seemed like one never finished a chore until other farming activities weren't just waiting; they were falling on top of you and covering you over. We did take time off for Sunday and other pleasurable activities which I describe later. Those fun times and school were probably the window that balanced the "all work and no play makes Jack a dull boy", philosophy. I don't think, I know there were not and are not any "lazy bones" in May and Rasty's offspring. In spite of the labor intensive farm work, we laughed a lot during and after work. It broke the monotony and set the stage for the next laughable event.

Mom and Dad's parenting, management and work styles were very different. Mom's orientation was that of a doer; get started and learn by doing; if you err or encounter a snag along the way, make adjustments, fine tune your approach and get the job done. Her "learn as you go" style was effective and accomplished a lot by the end of the day.

Just like May, I still like seeing where I've been and what was accomplished for the day, week, etc.

Dad's orientation was more like that of a thinker; it would be called strategic planning in today's world. He tried to assess the situation and think it through before starting a task or any long term endeavor. He was not methodical to a fault, but he did think and plan carefully. I could never figure out whether his planning efforts were purposefully drawn on to stall or defeat the chore/

project before he got started, or whether he couldn't bear the thought of finding a flaw in his planning. In any event, by the time he had it mapped out, Mom and her work crew could have finished that chore and moved on to the next two or three.

Dad was methodical and very mechanical in his thinking and parenting. Everything seemed purposeful and goal oriented. He moved from point A to point B one step at a time. It didn't seem very fluid to me. Dad had a short fuse which was easily sparked; didn't take much to set him off. Needless to say, we figured that out early on and just gave him lots of space and distance. If you weren't close by, you ran less risk of setting him off. I'll give you an example. One summertime day in 1946, I was on the screened porch searching through a treadle type Singer sewing machine for a needle and thread to replace a button on a shirt. The next two events happened simultaneously. I pulled a small sewing machine drawer out too far and dropped it on my big toe. It hurt, it really did! Try dropping a 5x5x15 inch wooden drawer on your toe. The drawer didn't go down flat. It was upright long ways and vertical. The corner of that drawer smashed my big toe. By the way, I was barefoot and the floor on that porch was concrete. That concrete floor had never heard of spring, relief, or give when something was dropped on it. At the same time I dropped the drawer, Dad arrived home from work, tired, sweaty, and I didn't know his mood. I did not know of his presence when the drawer dropped either. I was in pain, had grabbed my toe with both hands and was jumping up and down in a circle, not squalling or uttering any church words. I was just jumping on one foot and holding the wounded toe. Dad didn't say a word. He set his dinner bucket down,

4

stepped back off the porch, cut a peach tree switch (the worst kind – a long, water sprout, flexible and hurtful), called me off the porch and wore the switch out on my back. "Now you have something to complain about", he said. He picked up his dinner bucket and went into the house. I was left crying and confused. I wanted sympathy and comfort, not more PAIN. I don't think he saw the drawer drop; he only saw this eleven year old boy hopping around on one leg with some weird look on his face. He didn't like it, it set him off and I was a victim of <u>his</u> child rearing practices that day. Today his behavior would have resulted in him being removed from the home, sent for psychological evaluation, rehab, and perhaps family counseling before he was allowed back home. His behavior was over the top, even back then I must say. However, whippings were the norm then and neighborhood kids received similar punishment at their homes.

I have had seventy plus years to study and reflect on Dad's behavior and child rearing practices. I think I understand most of where this behavior came from. I will not elaborate on my analysis; however, I will say he provided a life-long character study which was very interesting indeed. I will also say I did not like or agree with his child rearing practices then or now. I can also say I learned a lot about human behavior from his behavior. He was most likely instrumental in my choice of a career; the study of human behavior. Thanks, Rasty.

Mom – Lilly May Annon Ball

Lilly May Annon Ball was born May 28, 1907 and lived until March 2000. Mom and Dad were married in April of 1924. They parented ten sons and one daughter. If there was ever a member in the Saints of Barbour County, she was in the front row. She not only took care of her own family, but helped neighboring families as well. For example, she cut their hair, made clothes, helped with canning vegetables, butchering, thrashings, washing their clothes and helped nurse the sick. Her war chest of medicines ran from kerosene and sugar for colds, Epsom salts for stomach, Fry's Worm Medicine for spring worming, Creolene for cuts and bruises, Sloan's Liniment for sprains and muscle aches, and all-purpose aspirin for anything else. She had given up on the asafetida bag by the time she doctored the younger kids. She just rubbed our spasmodic chests with rendered skunk lard and said, "You'll be okay". I think the okay thing was most helpful.

During World War II, Cod Liver Oil was the craze. One tablespoon for each child at bedtime was required to maintain good health. She gave it to "Rasty's three little shits", religiously every night. That stuff tasted awful and lingered in your mouth and throat all night; thick liquid, oily fish taste. That's why I don't like fish today. Occasionally she'd forget the Cod Liver Oil ritual. Cecil and I prayed, "God don't let her remember, please God". Guess what, there's always one AH in the crowd. Brother Hayward liked the Cod Liver Oil; must have been because he's left handed and a really bright kid, i.e., into healthy foods early on. As Cecil and I prayed for Mom to forget or go to sleep before she remembered, we would be bedded down for quite a while before Hayward would say in a loud voice, "Mom, you forgot the Cod Liver Oil". Cecil and I were disappointed that God didn't grant our prayer, but quickly changed our prayer to, "God forgive us for this murder we are about to commit". We thought about the murder, but didn't commit it. We didn't like the thought of hanging on the end of a rope. We let him slide one more time. Mom continued the Cod Liver Oil routine until Cecil and I told her to give our share to Hayward. And if any readers want to send Habie their leftover Cod Liver Oil, feel free; just promise not to put arsenic in it. That would be a dead giveaway of you having someone in your family who liked the stuff too. Hope you didn't kill them either.

Mom, like all good mothers, took good care of her flock. She managed more work details and projects simultaneously than most finish in half a life time. Her management style was by example. She wouldn't ask us to do something she wouldn't or couldn't do herself. From my perspective, all her children emulated that management style and she would be proud. She was the farm manager and knew what needed to be done and when. During spring planting through harvest, she kept her work crew on schedule. If it was too wet to cultivate or put up hay, there was firewood to cut, fence to mend, and harness repairs to be made. I hated this one; cut bean poles or brush.

Have you ever gone into the woods after a rain (or even during) to cut bean poles? If you have, you know when you emerge from cutting, with poles in hand, you'll look and feel like a drowned rat. You were not as wet as when cutting brush in the pasture field after a rain where you'd be wet from the waist down and have rip shin briars adding to the misery. Rip shin briars and wet pant legs work well together, but there was always Creolene.

Mom was well liked and popular in Barbour County. She was a great story teller, liked people and fed most Barbour Countians at least twice. Entertainment and fine meals, who wouldn't like my Mom? She kept people laughing and interested. What amazed me the most was her ability to relate to the young and the old; from young kids to senior citizens, all were eager to visit with her.

After the family work crew (her children) left the farm, she hired workers to come do the heavy farm work. However, she did all the light work such as gardening, feeding livestock, cleaning the spring out, and so on. Since she now had "free time" she started an "upholstering business" and she was good at it. Do it right, was her motto. She had chairs and couches in process all over the screened in porch. She didn't set and twiddle her thumbs; she enjoyed being productive. "What's next" was ever present in her outlook on life.

I'll relate two stories about Mom's farm management and sense of humor. Summertime meant she raised a half acre garden for canning and selling some vegetables. She took pride in <u>her</u> garden and was vigilant in keeping insects, weeds and varmints out;

raccoons, opossum, bugs, rabbits and deer were always plentiful. I'll speak first about the raccoons, those tree dwellers with the ringed tail and sporting a mask. They were cute, but destructive once they found the veggie banquet hall. Mom always inspected her garden first thing in the morning. She would check to see what was growing and flowering, what needed weeding and sprayed with Sevin Dust, etc. She made mental notes and would attend to each issue later. So far this particular morning nothing appeared unusual, but then she spotted tracks of a raccoon and evidence of his visit in a few corn rows. She then found where the raccoon had entered under the fence. Raccoons are pretty good at breaking the codes at Fort Knox I am told. Mom kept steel traps for such pests and knew how to use them; anchor the four foot chain with a stake or secure it around something, set the trap, place it in the raccoon's path, and BINGO! If he steps on it, he's caught! She was satisfied that she'd have him by the next morning. The evening and nighttime came and went. She was up in the morning to inspect the garden and was focused on the crop, walking and making mental notes. She forgot about the trap, stopped by the post with the trap attached, heard a noise and looked up. She was eye ball to eye ball with the raccoon sitting on top of the post. I don't know who was startled the most; however, she pointed her finger at the raccoon and said, "You wait right there, I'll be right back". The raccoon waited; he had one foot in the trap and nowhere to go. Mom returned with her trusted twenty gauge double barreled shot gun and there was a raccoon funeral before noon that day. He, nor his relatives, ever returned to the veggie banquet hall in May Ball's garden that summer.

Mom and her bountiful harvest.

Later on in Mom's life she used a cane to steady herself, herd cattle, whack the dog, and give a chicken in her yard one of those Cape Canaveral lift offs. At this point in time she lived alone and also carried the cane for her personal protection. I'll elaborate on one other use of that cane. Occasionally, mice would find their way into the house. Cats may have gone on strike or just missed one of those furry little devils with big teeth. She had heard and seen a mouse a couple of times in the kitchen. She set mouse traps, but had no luck the first few days. She thought that mouse had witnessed the raccoon's foot in a trap and his last rites given with the likes of a twenty gauge double barreled shot gun.

No Siree! No traps for me. Now the two of them were in a strategic war. Who will outsmart whom; Mom, the person in command of all activities inside and out, or the little mouse with big teeth that had just moved in about five days ago? When nothing else works there's always Decon. The Commander (Mom) spreads a few pellets in dark corners and under the refrigerator as it is warm there during those cold winter nights. Time passes. The second night after spreading the bait, the Commander is up at midnight sitting at the table munching on a snack; if you can't sleep, then eat. Mom's pretty alert for noises and sightings of things that are not supposed to be there. Well, you guessed it. The little mouse crawled out from under the refrigerator and staggered toward the Commander sitting at the table with her cane across her lap. She watches the mouse as it struggles to keep its balance. The mouse stops occasionally and looks up at Mom. As it gets closer it's trying to wave the white flag and surrender. True story. She said, "Good morning, you don't look like you feel so good". The mouse staggered on until he was within reach of her cane. It never knew what hit it nor do I know any details about the burial arrangements.

Mom lived until March 2000. She was within two months of her ninety third birthday when she passed away. She lived alone during the last dozen years of her life. She loved her cattle and mountain farm. Her great grandfather, John Annon, migrated into the West Virginia mountains from Londonderry, Ireland. Given his age, I would guess he arrived in the US during the late 1700's or early 1800's. Mom always said he had claimed the land and settled there as a "squatter". In any event, she was a fourth generation of the Annon Clan to live on one of the original Annon farms. We

11

were the fifth generation to farm that mountain top. Mom lived eighty three years out of ninety three on her home place. She was born and raised in the house her father (Henry G. Annon) built around 1880. I and three younger brothers, Cecil, Charles, and David were born there also. Brothers Carl, Harold, Donald, Hubert, Lewis and Hayward and my sister Betty were born elsewhere, but grew up on the Annon farm.

As a young boy/adult growing up there I did not have the interest or attachment to the Annon ancestors that I have today. I did know John Annon was from Ireland, had homesteaded on our mountain top and that he was buried in the Annon graveyard on our farm. Note the our. Even then I felt connected in some way to Ireland and ancestors. Today I visit with John Annon, his son Zachariah and his son Henry who are resting in the Annon graveyard. I like spending time there with them, often wondering about what life was like for those hard working pioneers; pioneers, who cleared the land, tilled the soil and raised families on the Annon Estate. I ponder my lineage. Did I inherit their craft, drive, stamina, abilities, wonderment and pioneer spirit? I hope so.

Rasty's Early Years
in Tucker County, West Virginia

Dad's life was not complicated, but he was. He was super strong willed and didn't mince words. When Rasty spoke, we and others listened. He spent most of his early years (1899-1910) in Barbour and Tucker Counties, West Virginia; deep in the Allegheny Mountains where times were tough and people were tougher. Dad, his parents, three brothers and two sisters, lived on a one horse, forty acre farm and scratched out an existence by farming, hunting, and gathering whatever was edible.

There were no entitlement programs during those days to assist with food, clothing, shelter or health care. They "made do" with what they had or could find. The only "cash" they ever held was from helping other farmers in their community or a few dollars from George Monroe Ball's Ministry. George Monroe was Dad's father, my grandfather. He was a circuit riding Brethren Minister associated with the Shiloh Church of the Brethren in Dantown, West Virginia. He would ride his circuit and hold revivals in other communities. It was not uncommon for the Reverend Ball to be gone a week or two, serving churches within a twenty mile radius. Saving souls was his mission. My question for the Reverend, what preparations did he make for the family before leaving Dora, "the wife" and five small children? Were there enough provisions left or did they fend for themselves? My guess is the latter. Dad didn't talk much about that although he did skirt the issue a time or two. One of his brothers did indicate that the Reverend didn't leave provisions for the family, but felt "the Lord would provide". In any event, the Reverend Ball would return with a few dollars, a full belly of chicken and other edible commodities for the family. Life was good until the next call came for the Reverend to mount the horse and ride off to save souls in the hollers and valleys of Barbour and Tucker County, West Virginia.

The Reverend rode out on his next mission truly believing, "the Lord will provide". Maybe the Lord did, but Dora (Grandmother Ball) and five young children were left to fend for themselves. Dad was almost ten years old and his brother Hobe was about eleven. They helped Dora take care of four younger brothers and sisters. They hunted game, tended one cow, one hog and twenty chickens. Dad said the most difficult task was finding, cutting, and dragging tree limbs from the woods for firewood. Dragging tree limbs through two feet of snow was difficult for a strong man and almost impossible for two young boys, but they did it. They then chopped the limbs into firewood length and managed to keep a fire going for the family.

Winters in the higher elevations of Tucker County can be brutal. I can only imagine how difficult it was to survive a winter in Tucker County. I wouldn't want to try, especially in a house with no insulation, furnace, weatherization or indoor plumbing.

I now realize why Dad did not want to talk about his early years in Tucker County. Those memories had to be too painful.

14

Rasty and Buddies – Guarding the Harem

I'm not sure if mountain peoples' customs are all that different than other rural locations. Also, I doubt that some mountain customs are written, decreed or declared; they just happen intuitively and serve as needed. This could get more complicated so I will just illustrate with a story, an example of "Guarding the Harem".

Dad always told this story with a chuckle in his belly as he was one of the young men (boys) involved. He and other young men would have been fifteen to eighteen years old and the year would have been about 1916.

"Guarding the Harem" is the custom addressed in this story. This custom involved young men in any small rural mountain community and how they would attempt to protect young women in their community from male intruders from the surrounding communities at school, church socials, revivals or family reunions where other community people were invited and would attend. If during these events a young man from another community became interested in a local girl, the local males would be vigilant with their protection; if it appeared the "outsider" was "too interested", the local young men would flex their muscles and invite the young man from another community to either leave or fight. The "outsider" would either remove himself from the challenge and leave, or accept the challenge and get involved

15

in a fight. Of course, the suitor would get his "clock cleaned".

Most of the locals knew that the strongest and quickest male would volunteer for the match. In most cases, the Moatsville defender was a young man named "Teet". He was stronger, quicker, more experienced and never turned down an opportunity to show his fighting skills. He did not lose.

On several occasions, the Clemtown boys had intruded into the Moatsville Community and were showing <u>too much</u> interest in the young ladies. This did not set well with the young men in Moatsville. They did not like the intrusion into the Moatsville Harem. Dad and the Moatsville boys met and decided they would go to Clemtown and teach the young bucks a lesson.

Plans were made, a date was set, and word was delivered to the Clemtown intruders. They agreed to show up at the appointed time and place in Clemtown. You can imagine the chatter and bragging about how the confrontation would begin and end. Each side thought they would "show" the other one who was boss.

Dad, Teet, Dowden, Hobe, Buck, a few Freemans and Ritters collected at Moatsville and started the trek to Clemtown; a five mile hike. Teet was the main volunteer fighter. He had bragging rights and was being complimented profusely by the others as they made their way to the battleground site. Dowden was carrying a lantern to light their way as dark would arrive before they reached their destination. The lantern would also light the battleground once they got there.

The Moatsville boys arrived and were pumped up for the confrontation. The Clemtown boys were ready and waiting. Lines were drawn and the signal was given; the fight was officially on. Dowden plunged into enemy lines swinging his lantern back and forth and was well into the Clemtown crowd. With fists flying and scuffling about, Dowden thought he had best check to see if his backup, "Teet", was behind him. He turned to look back and "Teet" was GONE! The rest was history. Dowden soon lost his lantern, got his lights punched out, and needed help to hobble back to Moatsville. The fight ended with a few bloody noses, scrapes and bruises. Of course the Moatsville boys thought they won; however, both sides won and both sides lost. It did quiet the pursuit of young ladies by the Clemtown bucks for a short while; however, further interest in the Moatsville ladies returned within a few months and bickering continued as usual between the two groups.

Rasty did say that Dowden's back up "Teet" lost a lot of credibility that night, especially with Dowden. Rasty and others did get involved as Dowden's backup and finished the fracas. As with any game, event, contest, etc., it proves you had best not put all your eggs in one basket. It goes better if it is a team effort. When Dowden looked around for "Teet" and "Teet" was GONE, no doubt panic was closing in on him. It provided many a good laugh and story for Rasty to tell.

From 1916 to the 1940's and 1950's, this custom was still in operation. "Guarding the Harem" was very alive and well in surrounding communities beyond Moatsville. Before I left the mountains in 1953, I witnessed many a fight and brawl. Matter of fact, I must confess that I participated in a few episodes of defending my turf or intrusions into another Harem nearby Testosterone creates so many problems for young and old alike.

"I looked around for "Teet" and "Teet" was GONE is a good expose on trust, disappointment, mob psychology, male ego, the power of testosterone, the courting game, rivalry, and friendship. I expect there are young men throughout small communities in West Virginia and beyond who have experienced "Guarding the Harem". I doubt it will be extinguished in the near future. Testosterone and the male ego are powerful dynamics. They have created the drive to risk life and limb and to master more than just creating babies. Think about it!

Blowing the Fecal Plug

It has been documented that bears hibernate for long stretches during the cold months of winter, and that their first priority upon awakening from that long sleep is to forage for new spring grass and other green plants to eat. This is necessary to cleanse the bowel after the long nap. It is called blowing the fecal plug. It cleanses the intestinal tract and makes ready for a regular diet during the summer.

Rasty's method for blowing the fecal plug was similar; however, he didn't eat spring grass or green weeds. Instead, he used a quicker method for cleansing the bowel. He ingested four tablespoons of Epsom Salt. The Epsom Salt box suggested two tablespoons. Rasty wanted quick and fool proof results; therefore, using four or five tablespoons full of the salt was always successful.

I always wondered if he noticed the skull and cross bones over the poison label on the box. The box plainly stated "contents are poisonous", keep away from children. If you have taken Epsom Salt you know that a regular dose moves everything in the intestinal tract within a few hours. No one, and I mean no one, had better be on the path to the outhouse or in the bathroom or you will get run over on the path or the door will be ripped off the hinges.

Ordinarily, Rasty (Dad) didn't get in a hurry; however, on <u>Blow the Fecal Plug</u> day, he could make it to the outhouse in record time! I believe he could have kept up with the Indy 500 race cars on <u>Blow the Fecal Plug</u> days. If there were any road hazards between the house and the outhouse, disaster was eminent. One such mishap did occur one spring morning after a good rain. This was his second round of Epsom Salt for the year. He took four doses per year. It was about mid morning when the stomach made its first flip; a signal that says get to the outhouse immediately! With 300 PSI boiling in Rasty's belly he was on the way.

There was a small drainage ditch half way from the house to the outhouse that he would jump over or take an extra long step. He tried the latter. At mid-point of that long step he slipped, did a split and fell into the drainage ditch. Since this was also free range for the chickens, ducks and a couple of geese, they had made numerous deposits to the contents of that ditch. With 300 PSI in Rasty's belly, the split and fall into the ditch <u>blew the fecal plug</u>! After that, he had no further need of going on to the outhouse.

After a few church words and any other expletives he could think of, he picked himself up and returned to the house. Needless to say he was not a happy camper nor did he smell like one. Not only had he blown the fecal plug in his drawers, but he had also received a bath from the drainage ditch; a two for one deal - plug removal and wallowing in the fowl droppings. This certainly added insult to injury.

When Rasty returned to the house, Mom was the only person left on the clean up detail; poor mom. All others in the house quickly vacated and didn't dare laugh at

Dad's acrobatics. We were out of ear shot before we released the belly laughs! We could not have kept a straight face as Mom had to.

There were other Epsom Salt episodes afterwards; however, none topped this one. I and others received Epsom Salt as a cure all. We learned quickly about Rasty's faith in Epsom Salt. If we complained about a stomachache, fever, leg cramps, etc., Rasty would give us a dose of that stuff. Believe me, it wasn't pleasant on either end. Who would want their innards turned inside out? No sir!

Even though it works to blow the fecal plug, I do not want or need to take Epsom Salt again. Would you? Read the label before you experiment with Rasty's Epsom Salt formula.

Doc Smith and Summer Inoculations

Doc Smith was the typical country doctor in appearance and patient care. He would see patients in his office in Philippi, West Virginia and make house calls to tend to patients and deliver babies.

Other than summer inoculations I saw Doc Smith one time in his office after a convulsion. I do not remember the visit, but was told years later by Mom that it was not a pleasant event in that I had bit my tongue in half; no wonder I talk different and can't sing the high notes. I mention this episode to indicate that mountain people did not visit a doctor unless it was beyond family medical remedies.

I remember Doc Smith and summer inoculations quite well. The anticipation and memories of prior inoculations didn't ease the pain and anxiety of what would happen on "vaccination day". For example, a girl older than I was waiting in Galls Store before Doc arrived. She was seated on a nail keg and became overwhelmed with the "to be" shot thing and fainted. I had not witnessed anyone fainting before; it didn't help prepare me for my upcoming shots. I had thought about skipping them this time; however, Mom took care of that and marched her flock next door to the Methodist Church. We were going to get shots for diphtheria, small pox, tetanus, typhoid, and whatever else Doc could stick you with that day. God, those shots hurt for a day or so!

Doc Smith would schedule his preventative rounds in each community during summer months; hot summer months at the Moatsville Methodist Church. Schools or churches in other communities were used. I am assuming the inoculations were the early years of public health as I don't remember any payment being required.

As early as I can remember, mid 1930's to 1940's, Doc Smith and his nurse would set up inside the church and use our skinny little arms as pin cushions. Of course, they practiced on all other kids and adults as well. Doc Smith was a typical country doctor; short, stout, granny glasses on the tip of his nose, gruff and sometimes impatient. However, he was revered and welcomed to each community. When patients visited Doc's office, he would usually recommend two to three pink tablets (probably all- purpose tablets) for three days and then give the pills to you. His patients followed his recommendation and recovered in a few days. He did not recommend "take these and call me in the morning". Telephones were not available in Moatsville and surrounding communities at that time. Ma Bell arrived after I was drafted in the Army in September of 1953.

Doc Smith was ahead of the curve in that he knew most patients would recover with or without the pink all-purpose pills anyway. I'm not sure if the pink tablets were placebos or not; however, they worked. His office calls ran from two to four dollars per visit. The all-purpose pills were free. And now for the rest of the story.

Doc Smith and his nurse started the vaccinations around 9:00AM and stayed until the last patient was inoculated. Doc wore the usual short sleeved shirt with that thing (stethoscope) around his neck in case someone fainted. Our vaccination day fell in the scalding July heat. Hot days and shots were not a good combination and someone young or old was likely to pass out. The nurse was in her white starched uniform and looked spiffy at first, but by the end of the day she looked a little bedraggled.

Doc and his nurse were set up inside the church. A small pan with alcohol, needles, a jar of cotton swabs, bottles of alcohol, etc. were spread on a table. We and others lined up outside and prepared ourselves for our round of shots. None other than the Mayor of Moatsville, Cheet, was in charge of crowd control. I must say his job was easy that day due to the fact that no one was too eager to get inside.

Mom and six of us would line up to take our turn. We learned from prior shots that needles were used and thrown back in a metal pan with other metal needles and when reused got dull quickly. Therefore, we tried to be on time and be near the first in line. Our turn at last! Doc recognized Mom as he peeped over his granny glasses and said, "Hello, May", asked about Rasty, then looked at us. Mom was the first to be inoculated and set the example of bravery for the rest of us. Bud and Major, our dogs, were watching this process. We followed her brave example and took our turn for the inoculations. Brother Don was about the second in line and stepped up for his shots. Doc punched at his arm two or three times before the needle penetrated. Doc's comment was, "toughest damn hide I've ever seen". Don was a tough kid. He didn't flinch or make a sound when Doc rammed four needles in his arms.

At about the end of our line one of the younger brothers got a shot and whimpered loudly. That set Bud and Major off and they came after Doc. Doc was wearing his pointed shoes and was located near the door. By the time Doc and the dogs had settled their disagreement, they were on the church stoop. When Doc got his last kick in, the dogs left for home. They weren't used to sharp pointed shoes and a nimble doctor.

Doc returned to his duty station and finished vaccinating the younger brothers. Doc didn't know it, but Bud and Major were doing their "guard and protect the family" duties that day. I was hoping they would close down the medical operation for the day; however, they didn't and I was next in line for shots. Doc stuck me pretty hard, mumbled something and finished up with brother Cecil.

While the Doc and dog fight was full of growling, barking and kicking, it didn't close down anything and we still got stuck. It did ease the pain a bit to see Doc do a weird dance and use a few church words I had never heard. I didn't know he could use that many church words in one sentence. Maybe it was because Doc was more educated and attended a more snooty church than we did.

After all the excitement we started home. The one mile climb up the mountain started with chuckles about Doc and the dogs, the weird dance, comments about our bravery, relief that it was over and that it would be safe swimming in the creeks and rivers. These feelings of relief and joy began to evaporate about halfway home as shots and a hot July day did not mix well. One by one we began to experience pain, upset stomach and turned pale and green. We had to rest more often and began to wonder if we would die from the diphtheria or tetanus shots. Perhaps a heat stroke would be welcomed to ease the pain?

We did make it in due time; however I really thought I was going to die on the spot many times during that journey home. The only high spot I remember from that day was that we didn't have to work for the rest of the day in the July heat. I expect we probably groaned and acted sicker than we were to stay out of the fields. In addition, our moaning and groaning won Mom's attention. She gave us a pat on the head and some of her homemade cookies.

Reflecting on Doc's defensive behavior, pointed shoes, and ability to continue his duties so quickly, it is apparent that he had encountered dogs before. His pointed toe shoes were worn for defense more than style, plus his quick steps and kick maneuvers were not that of a novice. A novice would have lost the fight with Bud and Major that day. Doc didn't lose his shoes or get his ankles gnawed off. Doc won that battle with two guard dogs fair and square.

After that fracas at Moatsville, Doc informed the communities to leave dogs at home for the day. Notices were posted about one week in advance of the community inoculation day. Shot seekers complied and left their dogs home thereafter.

In addition to displaying his defensive stance and quickness, Doc also showed local folks some of his tricky dance steps. He left Moatsville that day with a couple more positive notches added to his reputation as a fine country doctor. Thanks, Doc.

I didn't know until recently that Dad and Doc Smith knew each other during their childhood and remained good friends throughout their lives.

Grandpa Jones
Introduction to Bud & Major

Bud and Major, our dogs, were part of the family. While they were not officially invited to follow us to school, church, neighbors, swimming, a jaunt to the store, etc., they always tagged along. Perhaps they were on guard duty and we didn't know it. They did.

Will and Major 1943.

During the early forties Mom had planned to take us to see Grandpa Jones perform at the Moatsville Methodist Church on Saturday night. Grandpa was a radio star on the West Virginia jamboree in Wheeling. She thought it was an opportunity for us to expand our cultural horizons beyond the local entertainment. So on Saturday evening she invited any and all of us who wished to attend the show to go. The older brothers declined the offer. They weren't into Grandpa. However, Betty, Lewis, Hayward, Cecil, David and I tagged along to see the "show of a life time". Mom was such a salesman. We walked off our mountain top to Moatsville and arrived at the Methodist Church early enough to get seats on the third row.

At eight o'clock sharp, Grandpa, Ramona and a couple other band members began to play. They did a couple of fast banjo tunes, then Ramona and Grandpa sung a few songs. The audience was appreciative and applauded loudly. Most of those in attendance were like us; they had listened to the entertainers on the radio, but had not seen them perform live. As a matter of fact, I doubt that many of the folks in the audience had seen any "stars" perform live. It was the "real deal" and they were involved. It was a packed house and folks were enjoying the show.

About mid-point in the show, Grandpa chose his favorite song, "Here Rattler Here". The song, for those who don't know, was about calling old Rattler from the barn; a fast raucous song about Rattler the dog. Grandpa was singing at the top of his lungs and playing a claw hammer banjo to match. Little did he or we know that Bud and Major (the dogs) responded to the call. They came out from under the church pews growling and snarling and went for Grandpa's rubber boots. Grand-

pa never moved much during his entertainment episodes; however, he did that night. With dogs growling
and nipping at each leg, he danced, kicked and kept
playing the banjo. The audience thought it was hilar-
ious and part of the act until Mom got up and "called
the dogs off". She was embarrassed and tickled at
the same time. When the dogs were removed and the
dust had settled, Grandpa and the band members finished the show. Although the dogs added to the entertainment and were a crowd pleaser, no invitation or
contract was offered for them to join Grandpa's band.
He missed an awesome opportunity.

All in all it was an enjoyable show; a hallmark performance for Grandpa Jones and the dogs (Bud and Major). They walked taller and with proud tails pointing
skyward as they walked home with us that evening.
After all, they had stolen the show and were now celeb-
rities in the Moatsville community.

I expect other families in the Alleghenies have their leg-
endary stories about family dogs. We didn't own a car
so we walked to and from, place to place. Bud and
Major were with us wherever we went and that was
because we didn't roam very far.

I will include Bud and Major in other stories. They were
our constant companions and were regularly involved
in family activities.

Entering the Work Force

I was almost six years old on that typical fall day in September 1940. It was a beautiful morning, sun shining, crisp air and lots of dew on the grass. It was Saturday, potato digging day. Dad (Rasty) was home and in charge of the total operation. He had dispatched Harold and Don to borrow a horse, old Fred, from Uncle Jim. "And by the way, fetch the shovel plow as well." That meant they had to drag that shovel plow three quarters of a mile back home. They did. Everyone had a great breakfast. The usual sausage, biscuit and gravy (we should have franchised the biscuits, sausage and gravy before Hardees picked up on that one), two eggs, and of course fried potatoes rounded out the breakfast; coffee for the older ones, apple juice or milk for the youngest ones. Mom was such a marvelous cook. There were only ten of us around the table that morning. If I close my eyes, let my mind roll back in time, I can smell the hot biscuits and sausage. Yum.

As a six year old I was not into the hustle of that morning. I felt something was different. I just sensed something was going to happen and probably catch me off guard. Well, I didn't (then and still don't) like to be caught off guard or blind-sided. I must add at this point that Dad was not easy to work for. Reasons were, he didn't give full instructions nor was he very patient. I think he thought if he knew how to do something, then we should too. Nothing on a farm worked by horses and kids should be that complicated. However, for example, if he hoed right handed and you were hoeing left, you might get an ill comment, reprimanded, or cracked on the head with his hoe handle. That hurt! Heaven forbid anything would go wrong or tick him off. We always tried our best and gave him our undivided attention. Need I say his supervision style was far beyond a mean Drill Sergeant. Back to the almost six year old kid who sensed something in the air. That feeling was beyond all the brothers and Dad digging potatoes that September day in 1940.

Being a bit perceptive and independent as an almost six year old, I knew I'd better get a plan. After all, I was much too young to be in the potato digging operation that day. The plan – I would disappear - sneak away and spend the day playing at the Holmes' place. All I had to do was walk through the pasture field and drop over our mountain. Within ten minutes I would be out of sight and playing with Edith.

I was now working the plan. I had slipped away. Oh boy, oh boy! I thought, no one paid attention or missed a little kid. Kids were usually in the way, under foot, or asking for something, but not that day. I had covered about three hundred feet and not quite air born, when this booming voice called, "Wib, get back here". It took me by surprise, stopped me in my tracks and sounded like God had opened the clouds and spoke directly to me, loud and clear. I turned and shaking in my shoes (figure of speech as I didn't have shoes on), I walked back to Dad. He handed me a small galvanized bucket and said, "Here, you are going to pick up potatoes today". There was no discussion nor did I dare say,

"But, I don't want to".

That was my introduction into the work force; my first eight hour work day. It totally wrecked my plan with Edith, but I needed the experience for my resume and it helped elevate me to more important jobs on our farm. That introduction and other farm assignments prepared me at age eight to work for other farmers nearby. After that day, I belonged to every brother (usually the oldest) who supervised work on the farm until I was the oldest one left to supervise the remaining labor force. That was easy. I only supervised two; me and brother Cecil. David was too young for much supervision. He was a funny and fun kid. He is eight years younger than I.

We learned the work ethic on the Annon Farms that has remained with us throughout our work careers and beyond. I and all the brothers and sister Betty still use what we learned at home. Hard work and smart work doesn't kill anybody. I'm pleased that I was drafted in the work force on that September day in 1940.

Pictures

When I look at pictures, what I see is often more than just an image. I see the scenes, landscape, people, animals and birds therein. Some pictures cause me to remember that time and place. I laugh at some and others draw on the wellspring of my emotions. I often cry because I can't go back there. I do however remember the people lovingly and still have strong emotional ties. When pictures pique my emotional side, I let the feeling flow. I don't mind shedding a tear over these special places, people and things. They are a part of my being and deeply imbedded in my soul.

I have a picture of me taken by sister Betty during the summer of 1943 at Wells Falls along the Tygart Valley River. I was eight years old. Most would see an eight year old tow-headed kid standing on some flat rocks with the water behind him. I see an eight year old kid standing tall in his bib overalls, starched short sleeve shirt, and neatly combed hair. I see an eight year old with dirty bare feet firmly planted where he was told to stand. I look at this picture often; that eight year old looks back. I get tearful as my mind goes back to that time and place. It was a Sunday afternoon mid-summer. Betty and her date, C. H. Kelley, took me, Hayward, and Cecil to visit the Falls that Sunday. Wells Falls was named for the wells (holes in the sandstone that had occurred due to small stones washing around in a shallow or indented place on a flat rock ledge along the river). Over thousands of years, rocks and water can drill a hole in the sand stone. I see a kid who had never been to such an enchanting place; an excited kid; a kid in nature's wonderland. I also see a kid (like others) who didn't roam far from home. If it wasn't within walking distance, we didn't go. We rode that day probably seven miles one way. I also see an eight year old who was trying to understand life and where he fit in the scheme of things. I see innocence and I weep.

Will at Wells Falls -- 1943.

I weep for all kids at that time of life; a time of the unknown, a time of confusion, and a time of wonderment. A time to tell the world I am here, please understand me so I can understand.

I woke up this morning thinking about that eight year old boy (me) at Wells Falls in the summer of 1943 again. My mind went back to that day and time when that little "fellar" stood there proudly to have his picture taken. The world was very confusing and that kid was wondering where he fit in the overall scheme of things. Where would the winds of experience and time take him? At that time my world was very small and yet very confusing. Others appeared to have a place, a picture, or a plan for what lay ahead. I was totally lost in wonderment. No one ever talked to me about what was ahead and how time and experience would help me figure out who I was and/or what I would eventually become; and more importantly, that my development at eight years old was right where it ought to be. No one ever explained to me that if I would be patient, the future would unfold one day at a time. Intuitively, I knew to keep my eyes open, pay attention and learn about life and how to pick and choose. Decisions for an eight year old were difficult. After all, I had eight people above me who made decisions in reference to work, play, dress, social activities, and so on. I usually followed their lead; Mom, Dad, and siblings Carl, Betty, Harold, Donald, Lewis and Hayward. In addition, there were lots of older aunts, uncles, cousins and neighboring families. Even though I was insulated by a sea of family and friends, I felt very alone. I was left to stew in my own juices. In my youth, I and others rarely spoke about what was going on inside ourselves. Conversations were more about happenings outside your skin such as work, weather, time, place, people, activities, and sports. This contributed in developing a very private and independent personality. In looking back though, it doesn't appear to be healthy in that it kept part of the social development locked inside. For example, when was it okay to have a point of view and even more importantly, could it be expressed?

It was very easy to feel alone in a large family if your point of view was ignored. If ignored, your self-worth and personal value was compromised. Look at the eight year old kid again. Do you see his loneliness, confusion, and longing for a place at the "trough"?

Pictures are priceless. The older they get the better they become, although not everyone feels that way. For example, on a wall in our bedroom (two beds and six kids) hung a gilded framed picture of a stern looking man and woman. The man was seated while the woman was standing with one hand on his shoulder. Both were dressed in their best. I'm not sure who they were, but asked Mom one day, "Who are those people watching us?" She replied, "Oh, that's just some of the Moats tribe." My guess, it was my great grandmother, Katherine Moats' parents. Years later Mom was in a cleaning mood and had us burn the "Moats tribe" picture. I would cherish that picture today, considering it to be a good picture of our lineage and visible link to our heritage.

Bless my Mom, if it wasn't serving a useful purpose (her purpose), it was soon history. As those mountaineers would say, she got "shet of it". Obviously she didn't value that picture or the frame so she burned it!

Most folks cherish pictures and are eager to show pictures of a wedding, children, lost love ones, vacation snap shots, flowers, landscape, a new horse, and pets. I and you, if you are sixty or older, have set through an entire evening (3-4 hours) watching slides or real movies of a friend's vacation trip. It might have gone something like this:

First slide – "Here we are packed and loading up in the driveway." Car's pretty neat, luggage carrier on top, kids in back seat waving. Second slide – "Here we are back in the driveway, we forgot the cooler." "Here we are at the corner quick stop – needed to gas up and kids needed to pee." "Here we are at the neighbor's (usually a relative), dropping off keys to the house so they can water plants and feed/water the dog." It continues with shots at the camp site and explanations of each slide – the lake, falls, car trouble, Billy's poison ivy, Ally's swollen ankle, the campsite with smothering fire and smoke to keep mosquitoes away, and so on. After three to four hours, the slide show finally winds down. The last few slides – "Here we are back home". The last slide shows Mom and two children standing by a muddy car, bedraggled and "a not too happy face". Things are hanging out of the busted luggage rack, it's sitting sideways, and the trunk lid is now tied down and won't shut because we brought back more stuff. "Oh, here's Marvin with Rex, the dog; he was so happy to see us". You get the picture. By that hour of the night, I didn't want to see some dog named Rex slobbering all over Marvin. Would you?

Entertaining Rasty

The connection with the home folk and West Virginia dirt was and is deep within my soul and always will be. As with most mountaineers after they relocate, the magic and magnetic force of the mountains draws one home. It certainly takes me back to my roots. My wife, Doris, and I spent our formative years in Northeastern Barbour County - she from Valley Furnace and I from Moatsville. After we were married and moved to Ohio, Arizona, North Carolina and Indiana, we always made the journey back to West Virginia to visit our parents and relatives at least one to four visits per year with our children, Micah, Susan, and Donna. We felt they needed to visit the mountain relatives and stay connected to our mountain heritage. Our children loved those trips home and all the wonderment and freedom that farm life offered. Micah remembers getting in a little trouble by shooting chickens with his BB gun. Rasty, his grandfather, scolded him. When Rasty spoke, he listened. Susan and Donna also learned on a trip sometime later that when Rasty called you for breakfast, you were to get up then, not ten or five minutes later. He called them on one particular morning and they didn't get up. It was comfortable that cool frosty morning under grandma's quilts. Rasty returned and said "get up" and yanked the covers off of them. They were surprised, startled and "shook up" over the intrusion. They recovered quickly and were seated at the breakfast table a bit disheveled. There was no time for grooming or dressing for a fourteen and twelve year old that morning. You showed up and ate whether or not you wanted to. The girls and Micah needed that training and lasting memory. There were many more experiences with their grandparents that they now cherish.

I'm attempting to give you some sense of Rasty as a person. Yes is yes, no is no. There was no hem hawing around with Rasty.

I stated in one of my other stories that I had eighteen years to study, out guess, and practice mind reading while observing Dad's behavior. I thought I had him pegged and boxed up pretty tight; understood his thought processes and reactions to people and events until a visit during spring 1972. Doris and I went home without the children. They were old enough to stay alone. With Micah in charge we felt confident and left instructions that included the dos and don'ts, no parties, etc. We discovered later that they threw a party the first night. I'm not sure if there were more.

Now back to our trip home. I had thought this through. I was going to take some special entertainment to the folks back home, especially for Dad. I had seen Jerry Clower at a couple of farm/tobacco shows and was the proud owner of three of his long play recordings. I was getting into Jerry Clower and thought others should too. I was going to share "Jerry" with Dad and I did strategic planning to include records, an extension cord, and a small phonograph with detachable speakers that I borrowed from daughter Susan. I was ready and had instructions on the dos and don'ts. I had the entertainment loaded in the car the day before, but what about the luggage? I went back in the house, grabbed the luggage and off we went.

We arrived at my parents about mid-afternoon and unpacked. The usual "how are you?" and catch up stuff transpired. At five o'clock Mom and Doris were in the kitchen preparing the feast for six o'clock. Dad and I had the usual small talk, such as, any new guns and what's the wild game situation? You know; the important topics. "Supper is ready" came from the kitchen. Dad was on his feet and at the table. I had to hustle to keep up with him. Ordinarily he moved slow and methodically, but a call for supper was different. Rasty didn't miss meals. Plates, silverware, cup and saucer (he drank his coffee from the saucer), pass the biscuits and we're on our way. Not much conversation, just heap up the plate and eat.

During supper I asked Mom and Dad if they knew of Jerry Clower. Neither had. They did have a few new neighbors on the Tacy side; could that be Jerry Clower? "I don't think so," I said and explained "Jerry" to them both. Dad seemed interested, but Mom was not. She and Doris would clean the kitchen while Dad and I would listen to Jerry Clower. I set the phonograph up with the speakers set out for stereo sound. I slipped on the first "Jerry" L.P. and it began with the "Coon Hunt Story". Dad kept on wanting more volume. I had just about maxed out the volume on that pink phonograph; really, I had. I was enjoying the "Mouth of the Mississippi's" stories. Dad commented very little. I was really hoping for more than a half grin.

About halfway through the third episode of the "Ledbetters", Dad abruptly stood up and said to me,

41

"Shut that thing off, shut it off". "I'm missing my favorite TV program." I was stunned and disappointed. He stepped over to the TV, snapped it on, turned up the volume full blast, and we were now watching "Donnie and Marie". Dad's favorite TV program? "The teeth people"? (I coined the Teeth People term long before I heard it on any form of media.) I would have guessed that "Donnie and Marie" were about as far away from his taste in entertainment as one could get. I was floored! What had happened to Dad's acumen in entertainment? I had totally misread his interest in entertainment on that one. Hurt and disappointed, I did what the Arabs do. I folded and boxed the entertainment stuff and packed it in the trunk of the car that evening. After that, I did not take any more records to entertain the "Donnie and Marie" fan. Would you?

Red Ryders

Every boy wanted one, but few had one. During the late 1930's, early 1940's, there were two Red Ryder BB Guns staying with us. Brothers Don and Harold each owned one. Those Red Ryders were maintained and guarded just as much as Dad oiled and guarded his own arsenal. If for any reason someone moved, hunted with, or took one of Dad's guns off the rack, Dad would know and inquire as to who had his gun(s) down and for what purpose? His guns were off limits to any and all, period. Don and Harold learned that trait quite well. They weren't eager to lend the Red Ryders either. We could occasionally shoot one under close supervision, of course, by following gun care and gun safety. Then, and only then, we could shoot.

Don and Harold shot at targets indoors and out. I don't remember getting shot; may have been painful and blocked from the memory vault. They did, however, con brother Lewis into some kind of "manly experiment" where the stand down resulted in him getting shot with a grain of wheat instead of a BB. He even agreed to bend over and stretch his pants. He was confident it wouldn't hurt. After all, a wheat grain wasn't as heavy as a BB or as round and oblong; wheat grain would miss the target, his rear end anyway. The deal was set and ready. Lewis bent, Harold shot, and the wheat centered up on the target. It hurt! Lewis squalled like a stuck pig and got out of Dodge, so to speak. He walked and rubbed, walked and rubbed. He reconsidered his agreement and knew he'd been conned by two older brothers. He was not drawn into further bets again like "that thing won't hurt me".

Red Ryders early on were more powerful back then than they are today. Don and Harold's Red Ryders would shoot and kill small animals and birds. They thinned out the bird population and chipmunks, mice, and rats didn't fare any better either. We used a Sears Catalog for indoor target practice. No one got shot and all windows stayed in their frames. Those BB Guns would shoot through twenty or more pages of a Sears Catalog. Shooting today's BB Guns would not penetrate the front cover of a Sears Catalog and the BB would just bounce back.

I was covetous of my brothers' Red Ryders and not only wanted one, but <u>had to have one</u>! I was nine to ten years old and wanted to help keep the small animal and bird population thinned out as well. That was then, but today, no. All I could do was hope for a miracle as no money existed for a kid in the late thirties, early forties. Time passed and I still wanted a Red Ryder. I was twelve years old before I devised a plan on how to get one. I could earn fifty cents by selling one gallon of huckleberries. Gall's Store and I made a deal. Fourteen gallons of huckleberries would be seven dollars; the price of a Sears' Red Ryder. Huckleberry season was well on its way and I was ready. I was excited at last! I was going to have <u>my</u> very own Red Ryder.

For anyone who doesn't know about huckleberries, they are much smaller than blueberries. They are small native shrubs similar to blueberries. They are not cultivated, therefore they grow wild. Huckleberry bushes tend to find inaccessible rocky spots where nothing else is allowed to grow. They are not easy to find and more difficult to pick. If you're lucky, the berries will be up to a quarter inch in diameter. It takes roughly one hour or more to pick one gallon. That takes into account finding the berries and fighting with the bees and briars to pick your cash crop.

In addition, a farm kid didn't have the freedom to just find and pick them; he had to work during the regular day shift. Berry picking was done after regular work hours. I was lucky. Huckleberries grew on our farm with most of them located around the edge of a small patch of scrub brush and briars. All this was on a rocky knoll overlooking the Annon Graveyard.

It seems like I picked huckleberries every day for a month to make my fourteen gallons. I'd pick a gallon or two, deliver them to Gall's Store, then collect and save the cash. Pick and deliver, pick and deliver. I kept records of gallons delivered, gallons to go, cash on hand, etc. At last I had picked fourteen gallons of huckleberries and had seven dollars. I was proud and ready.

Now, on to the business transaction with Sears. I had never bought anything of this magnitude before; maybe candy, a drink or an ice cream. I knew nothing of shipping, handling, or postage. I had seven dollars. What else did I need? Would I have to pick another gallon of the "Hucks" for postage and handling? The end of picking season had come and I had been through that patch a dozen times already. Believe me, those berries had been picked over. I was "bummed". Mom saw my misery and came to the rescue. She helped me place the order. We enclosed the seven dollars and she forked over the forty five cents for postage. Off to the post office I did go and the wait began. I waited at the mail box every afternoon when I was near the house. We were usually working in the fields or the back forty. That made the anticipation greater. One week went by and no Red Ryder. In the middle of the second week I received a letter with a money order for seven dollars. The letter stated that they were sorry, but the Red Ryders were out of stock. Could I reorder it at a later date? I was floored and angry at Sears. How dare them to be out of stock! We ordered clothes, fabric, baby chicks, hats, coats, shoes, etc. and they always came through. I had to think and reconsider. No more orders from Sears for me! I went to Gall's Store and began the process of buying candy, pop and peanuts. I limited my expenditures to one round of those refreshments about twice a week. It didn't take Mom long to notice my spendthrift behavior. Four dollars of the huckleberry money went back to Sears for a pair of shoes. I had part of three dollars remaining and continued to spend on refreshments. It didn't seem very long until my huckleberry money was gone and I still didn't have a <u>Red Ryder</u>.

One day, sixty five years later, I marched right into a local Wal-Mart and bought myself two <u>Red Ryders</u>. Of course these were not the quality and velocity of the 1940 type Red Ryder, but it pays to never give up on a worthwhile goal.

Trapping and Hunting in the Alleghenies

During the early years in West Virginia, hunting for small and large game, from squirrel to bear and deer, was routine. Trapping for pelts to sell and fox and coon hunting at night were special occasions for hunters and dogs. Hunters spent nights on ridges and in hollers listening to dogs tracking and chasing a fox or coon. The hunters would brag on their dog and how he was the lead dog on the chase. In addition to bragging and listening, a pint or two of white lightening or other spirits was consumed. As a kid I always wondered why the hunt lasted until the first light of day. I learned why later on. It took time to sober up to avoid the wrath of a disappointed spouse. If a hunter arrived home at 1:00AM and said "Hello Sweetheart" in a joyful mood, she knew, and all hell broke loose.

My family would occasionally coon hunt, but rarely did the fox hunt. Our hunting was mostly for small edible game such as quail, grouse, rabbit and squirrel; these were the game of choice. Rabbit hunting was my favorite and given a good Beagle dog, you would usually bag a few. Saturdays during hunting season Rasty and five or six sons would hunt across several farms. Briar patches, open pasture and wooded areas were best. In the 1930's, 1940's, and early 1950's, rabbits and squirrels were plentiful. It wasn't unusual for our crew to bag a dozen or more rabbits or squirrels. We'd skin them and Mom would prepare the meat for our evening meal. Her culinary skills copied the tried and true methods; boil first, roll in flour, salt, pepper and fry. She usually made gravy with the squirrel. The first hunt of the season yielded a pilgrim type banquet meal; no Indians, just lots of food and a full belly. There were no complaints. Others in the Alleghenies hunted and feasted on small game as well. I don't think our hunting and feasting was unique during those days. Dad was better at downing the quail and grouse. Carl, Harold, and Don were good at it too. It went downhill from there; two reasons for this. One, the older brothers and Dad had thinned out the bird population so much, birds were hard to find. Number two, since they were scarce, the younger brothers weren't expecting to "flush" a quail or grouse. When we did flush a quail or grouse it took off so fast and furious it startled us and we couldn't raise the shotgun fast enough. It was a pleasant surprise, however, to actually flush some. I always liked seeing the grouse sail around the mountain. That made the hunt worthwhile. Quail usually didn't fly far and set down quickly. We just watched where they set down and flushed them again.

When we expected them to rise, we were ready. The adrenaline was toned down and if we were lucky we'd bag a few. The opening of hunting season was always exciting: up at 4:00AM, eat a big breakfast, plan the day's hunt (where each would hunt) and don't shoot at anything unless you were sure what it was, period. At noon time we'd meet and reorganize. Of course the hunting grounds had been scouted by a couple of older brothers. They took the prime spots and thought we didn't know. In addition, they usually tested their guns and bagged a few squirrels early; undercover, of course. They used twenty two rifles, because they don't make much noise.

Deer and turkey were scarce in our area, but a few were bagged during the regular hunting season. After the 1930's and through the 1950's turkey became more plentiful. It was not unusual for Mom and Dad to see a flock of turkeys within thirty yards of the house. The deer population also increased and was very visible. It made Mom furious when they visited and ate her garden vegetables. "Durn deer!" On occasion, she'd give them a charge of number four shot with her double barrel twenty gauge.

Trapping for prized pelts was one means of income for the Allegheny Mountaineers. This and free land brought people into those mountains before and during the early 1700's. I asked Dad what brought his relatives to the Alleghenies. He elaborated on two possibilities. The Ball side wanted to become frontiersmen or they had to leave Virginia in the dead of night. He didn't explain dead of night so you'll have to use your imagination.

The Reed side (Dad's mother) migrated from the Harrisonburg, Virginia area after the Civil War. Before the war, they were reasonably well off as they owned land and married into prominent planter type families. After the war their southern currency was worthless. They lost their bank holdings and land due to taxes. They simply couldn't pay. The Reed family relocated to the Alleghenies in Barbour County, West Virginia. My great grandfather Reed's goal was to recoup his status and wealth. The Reeds worked the mountain farm like all other mountaineers. They were good stewards of the land and active in church and community. Like other mountaineers, they added wild game to their daily menu and trapped for pelts to sell. They regained status, but not the wealth they had once enjoyed.

Trapping for us involved ownership (verbal) of a trap line, gunny sack, trap triggers, stretch boards, a sharp Barlow knife, and a place to hang and store the prized pelts. Of course you needed an assistant to help carry bait and traps and to help set the traps. The assistant thing was my introduction to trapping. On the first day of trapping season I would help brother Harold set traps on his line. His trap line was on the south side of our farm while Don's was on the north side. Brother Hayward was Don's apprentice. Both trap lines were approximately two miles long; up and down ridge tops, valleys, and anything in between. Steel traps were used sparingly and placed in a burrow. The most used traps were called "dead falls". Any trapper from the early days knows about "dead falls". "Dead falls" meant exactly that. They included a set of homemade traps, a post, a fly trigger and a bait stick. The trap was set under a large flat rock. The bait used on the bait stick started out with apples. Rabbits, possums, skunks and other small game would nibble on the apple and throw the trap. The flat rock would fall and end the bait stealer's life. The dead fall had done its job. After catching a rabbit it would be cut into small pieces and the apple bait would be replaced. Rabbit bait was preferred for skunks, weasels, minks and any other carnivores.

My apprenticeship in helping brother Harold involved skipping school and helping to carry traps, bait and most importantly, lifting the flat rock while he set traps underneath. For this seven year old boy's first time trapping experience, lifting a hundred pound flat rock was difficult. Harold would often help me get the rock up. This made it easier to hold it up until he set the trap and then he would help me ease it down on the trap triggers. I got stronger and better over the next few years at my lifting and holding apprenticeship and eventually inherited brother Harold's trap line while Hayward inherited brother Don's.

This occurred in the fall of 1942 or 1943. Harold and Don didn't want to smell like a skunk after starting high school. It was okay during grade school, primarily because other boys trapped and occasionally wore the skunk perfume as well. Hayward and I continued to trap and night hunt for skunks and possums until high school. Income from our catch, skinning, and curing pelts was used for clothes, Christmas funds, etc. Money for a skunk pelt ranged from a buck fifty to four dollars. Skunk pelts were graded from one to four. A number one was the pelt without the white stripe; just a dot of white on its head. A number four was the least valued. It had the broad white stripe head to tail. We'd gladly take a number four, because that was a buck fifty we didn't have. Possums were worth fifty cents to two dollars, depending on their size. There were other more valuable fur bearers such as minks and weasels. Brothers Carl and Hayward bagged minks. Carl caught the first mink I had ever seen. He caught it in one of the named fields on the farm. The Mace Field joined a spring fed run and was about three acres of tillable soil. Carl started walking his trap line one Saturday morning. As he started walking the trap line he spotted a mink under the dead fall. He hooped and hollered so loud everyone within two miles could hear the celebration. Mom said, "if he keeps that up he'll wake the dead in the Annon Graveyard". Needless to say, he was excited and was having a successful trap run.

Years later, in the winter of 1944, brother Hayward bagged a granddaddy mink. He may have been a relative of Carl's mink. It was a large mink and Hayward's greatest catch of all time. He did not yell and holler, but just came back to the house with a victory smile. After much fan fare, he skinned and stretched the hide. He later sold the pelt to a buyer named Hawk Shaw. Hawk bought pelts from other trappers in the area. The sale was made and closed with Hayward pocketing eighteen dollars. Most of the mink money was spent on a checkered black and red Woolrich Mackinaw coat. Dad talked him into buying one at least two sizes larger than his size. He wore that coat proudly and tried to "grow into it"; he never did. If he still has it after sixty plus years, it most likely would fit.

I'll finish this hunting and trapping story with two of my greatest catches. I caught the usual fur bearing skunks, possums and occasional rabbit for bait, but never a fox, raccoon or muskrat. Muskrats don't usually live or hunt on higher and dryer elevations. By the time I had served my apprenticeship in the trapping trade, the fur bearers were scarce. Ancestors and brothers before me had reduced the population to a bare minimum. However, many of those small animals showed their resilience and survived the wrath of hunters and trappers before my time.

My first noteworthy catch was a weasel. Weasels are small, slender, flesh eating animals; very similar to minks in that they are smart and difficult to trap. I don't think I outsmarted the weasel I caught on the Moats' farm; I just set a dead fall trap beside a cow path and had used rabbit for bait. Cow pastures in the mountains included brush and briar patches with some rocky and wooded areas as well. The trap I set included all the above. As a usual rule, animals large and small will also follow a well-traveled and worn path. The weasel had done that – followed the path. They also avoid anything that has human scent. I think the weasel used my trap because it had been set for at least two months and my scent had evaporated. I also think that weasel had forgotten all the safety rules. If it doesn't look like it belongs here, avoid it. He didn't get a second chance. I sold the weasel's hide for eight dollars.

My most memorable catch was on the Will and Nora Poling farm. Their farm joined ours and was located on the south side of the Mace Field. I had run my trap line late one afternoon and was within sight of home and the Poling house. Three more traps to go. One, two, three and done. There was nothing in number one; this trap was located under a cherry tree on top of mountains above the Poling house. Number two was half way down at the edge of the woods that had been cut years before. As I made my way along the edge of the woods I saw two things; a trap with something in it and Nora sweeping her porch. I was excited to check the trap and hustled down.

It was winter time. The leaves were gone so I could plainly see Nora and she would see me if she looked up. I was hustling to check the trap. I had walked the two mile line without a catch and was feeling really bummed. This catch was a picker upper. I didn't make any noise, because I was only about an eighth of a mile from the Poling house. I arrived at the trap, but suddenly the adrenalin rush was slammed in reverse and panic quickly set in. Think, Will, think. Nora's cat, a big orange, white and grey tabby was under the trap and still alive. Do I let it stay and come back later to release it? Do I raise the flat rock and see if it's okay? Nora was still sweeping. I kept thinking it through. For sure I had to make it past her house and disappear in the Mace Field woods before the cat got home or she spotted me. I wasn't into letting animals suffer. Dad always said, "put it out of its misery". I wanted to, but the cat might be alright. The plan: raise the rock and let the cat go. If the cat is okay, hit the trail home and hope Nora doesn't see me. If the cat has noticeable injuries, hide in the edge of the woods. Don't panic! I lifted the rock from Nora's cat. I was amazed how that cat had survived a huge rock slamming down on its head. The survival was not a good thing. The cat's head was very lopsided with the left eye two to three inches lower than the right eye and its head was wider than it used to be. When I raised the rock, that cat tried to walk or run. It would get on its feet and go left in a circle. While the cat's head had been flattened, it's orientation toward home had not been impaired. I was wishing it had been. It knew where the house was and tried to make it. The cat didn't squall or meow in the usual sweet sound they make when wanting to be petted. It made sounds of a low distress tone. By this time I was between panic and throwing up. I watched the cat fall, go in a twenty foot circle, fall, get up and go again. Think, Will, think. Do I go confess or do I disappear? I quickly chose the latter. I watched Nora finish sweeping and exited the area. As I was safely disappearing in the Mace Field woods, I heard Nora calling her cat. She had reappeared on the porch and was watching the cat's circling behavior. I chose not to wait for the real discovery of why her prize cat was making twenty foot circling maneuvers on his way home.

I don't remember resetting that trap nor did I ever hear of any funeral arrangements for Nora's cat. No questions were asked and no information was revealed. This exposé is my first confession. May Nora's cat rest in peace. Sorry Nora!

I don't think our trapping and hunting was unique or unusual for that time and place in the Alleghenies. Times were tough and so were the people that lived in those mountains. Growing up there was a great experience. I have often said I wouldn't trade my years growing up in the Allegheny culture with anyone I have met from other parts of the United States. God bless the Alleghenies and Nora's cat.

Night Hunts

I always had mixed feelings about night hunts for fur bearing animals or just the sheer joy of a coon hunt or fox chase. The greatest issue for me was that it was usually cold and damp and carbide lights only light up about ten feet in front of you. If some bull, horse, cow, bear or scratching type animal was in the area and we startled it, it could stomp, gore, or shred us on the spot. I never knew what was past ten to twelve feet ahead and that was not comforting. The only saving grace was the hunt dog "Butch". He would have warned us. Oh what a relief to know "Butch" was out there in the dark somewhere.

"Butch" was a great hunt dog. He would get excited when Hayward and I were making ready for a hunt. He knew that by about 8:30PM we would be off in search of possum, skunk and raccoon. We preferred skunks due to the dollar value of their pelt. The big issue with a dog and skunk in a stand-off fighting match and a light with little ability to light up the fighting area was getting sprayed. If you have ever been sprayed by a skunk, you know you will wear the "skunk perfume" for a few days. You wash often and try to mask the "perfume" with cologne, horse liniment, raw onions, or other concoctions, but most just don't work. After three to five days and lots of scrubbing with lye or Octagon soap, other kids would not turn up their noses and say "phew, what's that perfume you're wearing"? They "knew", because a brother or father wore the perfume from their hunts as well.

Brother Hayward had heard that if you picked up a skunk by its tail it couldn't use the protective spray mechanism. He just had to try it. On one of our hunts on the "Poling Place", a large cutover meadow, "Butch" cornered a large skunk. They were growling and circling each other. I held the light and was the referee and observer while Hayward was the adventurer and examiner of the theory "if you catch a skunk and hold it up by its tail it can't trigger the defense mechanism". All was going well. "Butch" was holding the skunk at bay; not too close to the sparring partner. After all, "Butch" knew about being sprayed and didn't want to be blinded. He also knew if he got sprayed he would not be allowed back in the yard for a week or so. He stayed his distance, growling and circling. The skunk was aware of the dog, but not too worried about the carbide light and two young boys in his area. The skunk was concerned with watching the growling dog in front of him! Hayward moved in behind the skunk on one of the dog and skunk circling maneuvers. The skunk had his tail pointed skyward and ready to unload at any moment; an easy target for "old lefty" (Hayward). When the skunk and dog passed, "old lefty" reached in and grabbed the skunk by the tail and held him skyward. He looked at me, smiled and said, "By golly, he can't do it". The skunk hung and rotated looking for something to grab. The skunk wanted to get even with someone. About three rotations on an outstretched arm were enough. Hayward was either trying to decide how to finish the skunk off or now that he had him, what was next? Somewhere in Hayward's decision making process he relaxed the outstretched arm and the skunk latched onto his pant leg. The skunk unloaded on Hayward! It seemed like that skunk had saved up for this specific occasion. Hayward got wrapped up in the "phew"! Not only were his clothes covered by the spray, his eyes were blinded too. He dropped the skunk and "Butch" and I finished it off. Neither "Butch" nor I received any further spray. The skunk had exhausted its entire defense load on brother Hayward. I collected the skunk, rifle, dog, and brother Hayward by the hand and started towards home two miles away.

There were two streams of water and a spring on our journey home. We stopped at each one for the blind hunter to wash his eyes. By the time we arrived back home, Hayward had regained partial vision, but was not pleased with the instructions on catching and holding a skunk by the tail. I think he ignored the fine print in the catching manual which instructed a skunk catcher to "never allow the skunk to touch the ground or grab anything like clothes, etc." Lesson learned – always read the fine print because the devil is always in the details.

We didn't skin the skunk that night. Hayward stripped on the porch and spent the next hour trying to wash the "perfume" off. We went off the next day to The Huffman Academy and didn't mention our catch; we didn't have to. Hayward's "perfume" still lingered. Another boy had been night hunting and received a shot of the skunk "perfume" as well. He and Hayward shared the aroma with the entire student body. Within twenty minutes it permeated the room for all to enjoy. Hayward and the other hunter became close buddies that day. They most likely compared notes on who received the most "perfume" the night before. They hung out together at recess and noon time while the rest of us played our usual games or gathered in groups to discuss, "Boy, I'm glad I'm not wearing that cologne".

Hunting and trapping in Barbour County and the Alleghenies was not unique to us. It had occurred long before we arrived on the planet. It provided some income for anyone willing to run the risk of getting sprayed. In our area, skunks were not the most prevalent, but were usually the money maker. While minks and weasels brought more money, they were scarce and harder to catch. Possums were more plentiful, but less valued. We caught and skinned them anyway. A dollar was a dollar and a large possum pelt would sell from one to two dollars. After Hayward recovered from that night hunt, he was more careful and <u>never ever</u> picked up another skunk by the tail. We continued to night hunt for about another year; after that he was off to high school. He noticed girls and turned his attention toward them and academics. He later entered college, earning undergraduate and graduate degrees in Biology. Hayward retired several years ago from a stellar career in teaching and has continued his interest in Biology and nature. He is without a doubt one of the sharpest naturalist I have ever witnessed. Go on a nature walk with him and find out for yourself! He will give you the "Genesis to Exodus", "Alpha to Omega" on every plant, bird, tree, moss, and/or any creature in the pathway from the common name to the Latin name. He's a very knowledgeable individual and a great storyteller. He has lectured and guided nature walks in southern Ohio; very detailed, believable and informative. I suspect that "Butch", the skunk, and I were instrumental in helping him pay attention to the fine print and instructional details.

Snakes

Snakes have always fascinated me as well as scared the daylights out of me. Frankly, I can't say I like them nor do I like to be surprised by them. If I see them before they see me I am okay. Years ago on the farms in Barbour County, West Virginia, if anyone saw a snake and it had a head and tail, it was considered poisonous. It was therefore, shortly beaten, stomped on, clubbed, chopped in little pieces and sent on to snake heaven. I personally do not wish to ever visit there. I think I've had some nightmares about snake heaven and they were not very pleasant. Fact of the matter, they scared the bejesus out of me and it took me a couple of days to get over those nightmarish episodes.

Mother May was extremely afraid of snakes. If she saw a snake, she wasn't hysterical or didn't let out a blood curdling scream, but was more practical with her fear. She was scared, yes, but she kept her composure and chopped the serpent into a thousand little pieces! If a piece moved, it was cut in half again. She always kept hoes handy; one here, there, and everywhere. She was vigilant and not too many snakes crossed her path. Farm buildings were great havens for snakes. They are smart and know where small rats, bats, toads, and other little creatures like baby birds and rabbits may reside. Mom spent eighty three years of her life on the Annon Farm. She was born there and died there. She had plenty of time to know where to look for snakes and didn't miss many.

Mom did however miss one large black snake. One of the cats found it and brought it to her and placed it in the house. At that time cats had free run of the house. There were no screen doors. The cat sneaked the snake in while Mom was in another room and laid it under the kitchen table. When she returned to the kitchen, she didn't see the cat or snake until she heard a movement. When she saw the snake and cat under her table, enough was enough! She grabbed a broom and tried to kill both. She wasn't sure which one brought the other into her house, but she was going to murder both of them, then and there. I wasn't around to see or hear the commotion, but I'm sure it was a blur of swats with the broom and a few choice words for the cat and snake. The cat escaped with its life, but the snake was finished off and disposed of on a burn pile. Cremation was Mom's way of finishing "the bastard" off and knowing he wouldn't be back. I feel certain the snake welcomed cremation after a thousand mortal blows with the broom.

I don't remember the cat coming back after this incident. It is probably still running after being clubbed with the broom and may even be still confused about being punished for bringing in such a fine trophy for Mom. As a result of this fiasco, screen doors were shortly installed and no cats were ever allowed in the house again. Mom continued her war on snakes until she passed away in March 2000. She ultimately discovered that her 20 gauge double barrel shot gun was quicker and more effective in exterminating snakes.

My first <u>real fear</u> of snakes happened when I was about five years old. One of my regular chores was to gather in the eggs. I'd be dispatched to the chicken house twice a day; around noon and then again late evening. On one of the noon collections I decided I'd sit in a chicken nest and watch the chickens cackle after they laid an egg. So I climbed up in a corner nest and sat in it. Nests were nothing more than a shelf with eighteen inch square boxes that provided chickens privacy and peace of mind. I sat in the corner nest for quite a while and watched a white leghorn and a dominic red hen. When they finished laying they would stand up in the nest and cackle (poc-poc-pockak). Then they would hop down to the floor and strut off. I was fascinated. While I was studying the laying behavior, practicing the cackling and wanting to practice the chicken strut as well, I was interrupted by a visitor. My observations were nearly over when I saw dust falling down the corner above me. I looked up and there about three feet above me coming down the wall was a snake. It startled and frightened me so bad that I panicked. I froze and could not get out of the nest! I started screaming and the snake just kept coming. Guess what? That snake kept getting larger and larger and now it was going to swallow me! I knew that snake came to the chicken house to feast on eggs, but nevertheless, I believed that a ten foot snake with a hinged jaw would have no trouble swallowing a five year old kid. I was totally at the mercy of that snake. I thought one more foot and I'd be lunch for that ten foot snake! I kept screaming as loud as I could until one of the older brothers came to my rescue, pried me from the nest, and killed the ten foot <u>garter</u> snake. End of discussion for the brother. I was still scared and shaking when I got back to the house. I felt like that was a real close one for me. I had nightmares about that devil for years and naturally, the brothers teased me about it for years. After a week's vacation from my egg gathering job, I returned. I did not tarry in the chicken house nor did I have any further interest in studying laying behavior or poultry science as a career. Oh, and I never considered Herpetology either!

I have one additional story about snakes before I start shaking or start having recurring nightmares. In our corner of Barbour County there were several species of snakes, more non-poisonous than poisonous. Copperheads and rattlesnakes were there and avoided at all cost; there were mostly copperheads in our neck of the woods. The Annon Farm was a typical eighty five acre mountain farm with plenty of rocky areas, woods, meadows and pasture fields. My parents had plenty of farm laborers (us) and tried to maintain all eighty five acres. One of many maintenance jobs was keeping brush down in pasture fields, such as cutting briars, tall weeds, and small bushes. On one brush cutting outing brothers, Don, Hayward, and I were cutting brush in and around one of those rocky spots on the farm. Some of the rocks in that area were large flat rocks with small ledges underneath. For some reason, we brought brother David along for this particular morning brush cutting outing. We had all the tools and a plan to clear the area. David was only two years old. Brother Don carried him down to the area and placed him on a large flat rock with a ledge on the lower side. He had brought David a few toys to play with and he was to stay there while we worked. Can you imagine a two year old boy staying on a rock very long? Brother Don asked me to check the ledge for snakes. I've wondered since, if he knew. Like any responsible worker, I did what the supervisor requested. About half way around the rock ledge I spotted a large copperhead snake. I was about two feet away and was surprised. Finally, I was able to back off and tell Don and Hayward, S-N-A-K-E. Hayward picked David up and brother Don took care of the snake. We usually took a loaded gun for such occasions; you never know when a gun will be needed.

Hayward took David back to the house and returned. We worked until noon, took our dinner break and re-turned about one o'clock to continue the job. For some reason, Cecil came with us to work on the brush that afternoon. He was eight, I was ten years old and we could pile brush. When we arrived back at the work site, I wanted to show Cecil where we found the snake. He was all eyes and ears, interested in learning more about what we discussed during dinner. I proudly walked up to the ledge, talking to Cecil and embellish-ing the story a bit, then pointed to the spot and said, "Here's where the snake was." When I looked down my finger was within two feet of a coiled copperhead. That was a close call! We backed off and brother Don bagged his second copperhead for the day.

Apparently there's some truth to the story that where you find one copperhead there will be another one. From that day forward we always checked the area carefully, nor did we take brother David to the fields with us. We continued to cut brush during the summer and were more vigilant in getting rid of snakes. You never know where the next snake might be. I suspect other Alleghany Mountaineers have their own snake stories and could easily top mine.

Cider Kegs and Wine from a Jug

Dad always made cider and wine. During the 1920's, 1930's and 1940's, apples were plentiful. The tree diseases and insects later destroyed the older standard apple trees. Henry Annon, my Grandfather, had planted those trees in the early 1900's. Cider making died a slow death as the trees ceased to bear fruit. In the 1930's and early 1940's, Dad would have Carl, Harold, Don and Lewis pick apples; mostly shake them off, pick them up, load them in a pickup truck and take them to Mitchells Cider Press in Clemtown. I hope they sprayed them with water. They certainly weren't peeled or carefully graded. Dad, Harold and Don loaded the apples in Ding Wright's pickup and took them to Clemtown to have the cider made. Brother Don's recollection related the following: The driver, Ding Wright, Dad, Harold and Don arrived at the Mitchells about dark. Chickens, guinea hens and turkeys were already roasting on ceiling joists above the cider press. Dad and Ding Wright entered the shed, pulled off a burlap cover, dusted off the press and pulled it outside. I'm not aware of further cleaning or sanitation measures. Use your imagination. They fired up the apple press. Don and Harold used shovels to feed the press. The apple juice went from the press into the barrel. I hope they threw the first few gallons of cider away. They turned and squeezed juice until about two o'clock in the morning. The end result was fifty five gallons of raw cider in a whisky barrel. Dad would add a fifth of whiskey, or two, to the squeezing for flavor. I really think it was to purify the poultry droppings and crushed worms in the apples. Apple cider goes through a process of fermentation from sweet to hard cider to vinegar. I liked the fermentation/bubbly stage best; sweet and with a champagne taste.

Most farmers made cider and would always serve it to visitors. They visited each other frequently and would comment on the quality, color, and taste of the cider. They visited more frequently as the cider hardened. It had more kick and they stayed longer. Their journey home took longer as well. A carbide light or a two candle power lantern didn't light the foot path very well and a swimming head with little light slowed the trek home considerably. Dad never revealed the recipe; he just let them enjoy the cider. I think he also had more visitors. See "Green Apple Quick Step" (Appendix).

So now, moving on to wine making. Dad made wine early on and was quite good at it. Some of his ingredients were questionable, such as Polk berries in a batch or two. I've always heard that Polk berries were poisonous. He'd throw in some yeast to speed up the fermentation. Usually he'd leave out the additives and use tried and true wine making methods. I don't think his experiments with wine worked very well at times; for example, placing bottles or jugs of wine in the loft of the cellar house for heat to build up and speed the fermentation process. Give Rasty a point for that! However, he also soon learned the physics of heat and fermentation. The heat accelerated the fermentation process so fast it built up gas in the bottles or jugs and they exploded. He was left with very few jugs of consumable beverage. He figured that process out and made sure corks and jug caps were loose enough for gases to escape.

Dad's best wine making method was to squeeze the berries, grapes, and fruit juice into a ten to twenty gallon sized open stone jar and use cheese cloth to cover the top, allowing it to ferment. Blackberries, grapes, cherries, etc. were plentiful in Barbour County during the 1920's to 1940's. Dad would make a batch in the stone jar and test it religiously after his work day. A particular episode of Dad's tasting, testing, and sampling by holding the wine in his mouth for a minute or more, then swallowing, happened before my time. Brother Carl witnessed this event and loved to relate the story. Carl was very observant and watched the event unfold.

Dad arrived home at the usual time. He had supper and engaged in the "nothing unusual" type conversation. Dad asked Carl to get a lantern and go with him to check (taste) the wine. It was already dark and the lantern gave only enough light to "get by" without falling over something. Off they went, Carl about ten years old and Dad about thirty six. The mix was located in an open room over the cellar. Dad had a small glass stashed by the wine vat for the sampling and tasting. They saw where half the cloth had fallen into the wine mix, half intact. Dad raised the cloth and dipped the glass until it was half full. He did the usual taste test, swishing it around in his mouth, holding it and then swallowing. Pretty good, he thought - reckon not much longer before bottling. He went for a second taste test. He opened up the cloth cover a bit more and noticed something in the stone jar that didn't seem right. "Carl, hold the lantern higher." Dad removed the cloth completely. To his surprise a chicken's head was just visible above the wine. The chicken apparently fell in the mix earlier that day, got crocked, and died on the spot. Dad didn't finish the second taste test. He gagged and stepped outside to upchuck. Carl said the dead chicken head just bobbed up and down like a cork on water. That would have certainly given my stomach a turn or two. I don't know if they ate the marinated chicken or just burned it as a lesson for all the other chickens to stay out of the wine vat!

Rasty continued his wine making and became much more cautious about guarding his batch. He also got better at making it. His wine stood the test of all neighbors and visitors with whom he wished to share. Not all visitors were fortunate enough to receive a glass of his wine. He had total charge of distributing his stash. About midway in his wine making career he purchased a thirty five gallon oak barrel that had contained wintergreen from the Myers Clinic in Philippi. He used the oak keg for storing his wine after the fermentation was completed. Wine from the keg had the wintergreen flavor for years. The keg's bung was on the side, meaning it had to be stored with the bung plug top side - easy access for a siphoning hose to draw out wine. Dad had a small siphoning hose which he kept secured. No one used the hose; only the wine maker. He'd draw a glass for himself and neighbors, then replace the hose. Little did he know or suspect that young boys, 10 to 13 years old, had their own siphoning mechanism. Brothers Harold and Don made a twenty four inch reed from an ironweed stem, hollowed it out and used it for wine testing each morning when they went to the pasture field to bring cows in for milking. They looked forward to removing the bung and taking a draw each day.

In addition to that ritual, Harold and Don experimented with seeing how much wine it took to get me and Cecil drunk. Can you imagine giving a glass or two of fermented wine to a two and four year old? They did. I don't remember the second glass and I don't think Cecil at two years old remembers the first glass. The wine didn't take long to hit two little kids. Don and Harold had started our drinking binge at about four thirty in the afternoon one particular day. Cecil and I were sprawled out on the living room floor, sleeping it off by the time Dad arrived home from work at six o'clock that evening. He walked in and asked Mom about us. Her reply was, "they are just tired". She knew, but didn't say. She covered for the wine distributors. Harold and Don dodged another one. Thanks Mom. I do remember this wine binge, but it's a fuzzy memory at best and not recommended for a two and four year old.

Later on Dad bottled the wine in gallon vinegar jugs and kept them on the floor in the cellar. Any given day there were ten to fifteen gallons of aged wine on the floor in front of the shelves that stored canned garden vegetables. In order to take canned goods from the shelves, you would have to lean over the wine jugs and brace yourself with one hand on the shelf, then pick up the canned vegetable and stand back upright. This was inconvenient, but doable. Mom always canned and usually had three to four hundred quarts of canned goods on hand to feed anyone who showed up for the day or weekend. She remembered the depression years and was determined that no one would go hungry on her watch. Any given day during my early years on the farm she'd feed us (6-8 youngins) and two to four others who were helping or just passing by. It took lots of food.

I'm going to fast forward now and describe an event that took place with Mom, Dad and Fred. Fred was a son-in-law at the time; a great young man. He and I would challenge others to a basketball game, work together on occasion and often visit back and forth. On this occasion, we went to Charlestown, West Virginia to pick up furniture that his parents had given him. It was winter time, mid-February, and there was lots of snow on the ground. The roads were a bit tricky, but safe if you were a decent driver.

We arranged the time, day and overnight stay with Fred's parents, Ethel and Big Dave (a Retired Army Colonel). We arrived late evening the first day out. All the greetings took place; there was coffee, sticky deserts and discussion of the latest family events. The next morning we loaded furniture and continued on to Moatsville where I had two antiques stored with Mom and Dad. This is getting long winded, but I'm coming to the meat of the story. Hang in there for a few more paragraphs and a dangling participle!

The trip from Charlestown to Moatsville, West Virginia was more treacherous. We were going deeper into the Alleghenies where it was colder, with more snow and ice, and the roads went from four lane to two lane and then to gravel or mud. It was a gorgeous moon lit night, but very cold. We arrived around ten o'clock that evening, shared the usual greetings, and caught up on family and neighborhood happenings. You know, the standard stuff. By eleven thirty we were bedded down and drifted off into never never land. At about four o'clock in the morning, I overheard Mom and Dad in the kitchen talking. I couldn't make out the conversation, but knew something unusual was going on. They got up early, but not at four o'clock in the morning. I pulled on my clothes and went to investigate. They were discussing problems with the well; sometimes water, sometimes just a trickle, then nothing. The three of us decided we needed to check on the water pump in the cellar. The old saying "you don't miss the water until the well runs dry" was certainly appropriate in this situation. I thought this would be a good learning experience for Fred. I went back to the bedroom, woke him up and suggested he come and help solve the problem. He sat up and said "ok". I left Fred and joined Mom and Dad in the cellar. I asked them to describe what the well pump was actually doing; what it sounded like; when did this problem start; had it ever totally quit, and so on. It seemed to me to be an electrical problem. I asked where the source of electrical power came from and Dad pointed to a one bulb ceiling light with an on/off pull cord. I suggested we start the examination there. We did and found a connecting wire with a loose screw and tightened it. Fred then appeared as we were doing the repair, half awake, but wanted to be part of the celebration. Mom had retreated to her kitchen to prepare a country breakfast.

Dad, Fred and I stayed with the pump to check if it would build pressure and stop; the usual checks. By now it was a quarter of six in the morning. As we turned to leave, Dad said, "Would you like a glass of wine?" I was surprised; we'd made the wine cut list and he wanted to drink wine at six o'clock in the morning. I said, "Isn't it a little early for wine?" He said, "No", and then began the selection process. He selected a gallon jug. "This is a good wine. Here, hold this" and he gave me the jug. He then leaned over the wine on the floor, braced his left hand on the vegetable shelf and reached behind the canned goods and retrieved a hollowed out Ironweed stem about twenty inches long. He told me to remove the corn cob cork and I did. He then plunged the stem into the wine jug and said, "Take a draw". I immediately turned to Fred, gave him the jug and said, "Fred, you should go first". He took a draw, smacked his lips, and gave the jug back to me. I took my draw and gave the jug to Dad. He took a long draw, replaced the corn cob cork, set the jug back in its spot and then replaced the Ironweed stem. We went in for breakfast as our mission had been accomplished.

After we ate a hearty breakfast and loaded the antiques, we said our goodbyes and left. As we dropped over the mountain top and headed down to Moatsville, I said, "Fred, there's two things you need to know concerning what just happened back there." He was pretty alert and well fed at this point. "First of all, if you would have gotten up on the first call and helped solve the well problem, you would have been a hero here for the next two to three weeks". "Second, do you know why I gave you the wine jug for the first draw?" "No", he said. "Think about it. Did you see where that Ironweed stem came from?" "Yes", he said. "Do you know how long that stem had been there?" "No", he said. "Do you have any idea how many spiders and other critters you sucked out of that stem?" Fred sat quietly then began to turn pale and have a churning stomach. He needed to stop at the bottom of the mountain and walk around a bit in the cold. It took a few minutes for Fred to recover. He learned two things that morning. One, to take advantage of any chance to become a hero and

Two, don't ever go first if you're drinking homemade wine through a hollowed out Ironweed stem. By the way, that blackberry wine was one of Dad's finest. Fred may have learned a third lesson. Be on guard if he wanted to stay ahead of his father-in-law.

Barbers and In Home Hair Cuts

Have you ever had an in home haircut? I've had hair cuts from an in home, self-taught barber of three types: the barber who is gentle and gifted in gab and cutting; the barber who was not gentle, nor gifted in cutting or gab; and the barber who gave better haircuts than a regular barber.

During the 1920's to 1970's and probably beyond, most folks in our area, the Alleghenies, got haircuts at home. I'm not sure if I should call them haircuts or just hair removal. In either event, the hair was removed. Those home grown self-taught barbers were not into style; "a little here, a little there", style wasn't mentioned. You just went for a haircut and what you got was what you lived with. I remember boys wearing hats throughout the summer months after haircuts. That was before the popular hat thing today. Maybe we set that trend and didn't know it.

Mom was the gentle, gifted in gab type cutter. Early on she used the grip type clippers, a comb and scissors. She'd set us on a chair or stool, wrap the cutting cloth around our neck and shoulders, pin it and begin. She rarely allowed the handheld clippers to pull your hair. She would talk and cut and tell us to move our head right or left, up or down. She would often tell me two things. First, "You look and act (disposition) more like my Dad (Henry Annon) than any of the other boys." Mom would say what she was thinking without much thought of the impact on anyone else. While I was a young boy, I was proud to resemble Henry. I didn't boast or ever mention her comment about me and Henry to any of the brothers. I was just proud to be like Henry. She would put the "finishing touches" on the haircut with comb and scissors, then brush and comb my hair and pat me on the head. She was proud of a fine haircut and I felt lighter.

The second thing she'd say to me, not as often as the "Henry conversation", was that seventh sons were destined to be doctors. I was proud to be a seventh son, but the doctor thing was a galaxy or two out of the realm of possibilities. After all, I was still at The Huffman Academy learning simple elementary Math, Science, and West Virginia History. I was only in fifth grade.

Mom's barbering extended out to the community. She cut everyone's hair within a two mile radius and beyond. Of course she was gentle. She would cut hair and catch up on all their family news. Folks always knew when to arrive; suppertime. They got a free meal and a free haircut! If she'd had a full day, even in the middle of canning, etc., they'd still show up for a free haircut and supper. I have heard her say many times, "Here comes the Price tribe for haircuts." They were relatives and neighbors. She would spot them as they popped over the brow of the mountain. They would arrive, she would cut, they would eat and everyone left happy. We didn't have to wear hats after Mom's haircuts.

Dad, the barber that was not gentle or interested in conversation, fit the second barber type. He would throw the cover over your shoulders, you held it around your neck and he would begin. He must have gone to barber school to learn how to make the grip type clippers pull your hair. God that hurt! When he'd yank those clippers down or back and up, it left a place he didn't have to cut. There was no scalp or hair left there. It was bound up in the clippers. For the life of me, I couldn't figure out how he or anybody could get scissors stuck and yank them out with hair attached. He could and he did. Was he into the pain thing?

During the hair removal (roots and all), he would not ask you to turn your head right or left, up or down. He would take his hand, which was big and strong, place it on top of your head, grip down and twist your head sideways about one hundred eighty degrees. I think that's why I have neck problems today. Once the right side was cut, he'd repeat the hand on head, grip, and spin thing. I wonder if the Exorcist movie writers got part of the script from those haircuts. In any event, we should count our blessings that our heads were only spun around one hundred eighty degrees rather than three hundred sixty. Dad was not gentle! John Price and other "cuttees" can witness that "not so gentle" thing. We all learned to pick haircut days and times carefully. We preferred Mom's barbering over Dad's and never chose Saturday when Dad was home.

Now, on to the third type of in home haircuts; mine. I have, but do not like to, cut hair for others. Remember the open door barber shop on the Annon farm? Once it starts it only expands; more customers, more complaints, regardless of the free haircut.

I have been cutting my hair since the 1950's. I've had lots of good cuts and some not so good, but I'm getting better though. I've had one "store bought haircut" since I started self cuts. When my daughter, Susan, got married, I figured I needed to look sharp to stroll down the aisle and give her away so I went to the barbershop. I told Ray, the barber, "regular cut, nothing fancy like styling, etc., just a haircut". "Oh, and by the way, Ray, I have a large mole on my neck so be careful when you shave my neck." He cut the hair and then lathered up my neck. He shaved the neck, forgot about the mole and cut it off. I bled like a stuck pig. He slapped some stinging stuff on the root of the mole and placed a large band aid over it.

One day later, I'm strolling daughter Susan down the aisle with a "bollixed haircut" and a three inch band aid sticking out from under my shirt collar. I didn't feel sharp at the wedding, nor have I been back in a barbershop since.

I cut my own hair. I save a ten minute drive, a thirty minute wait, and more importantly, my cuts are better, plus I get to keep the mole on my neck.

You take your pick. Which barbers do you want?

What's My Name Anyway?

During the 1920's through the 1950's, large families in the Alleghenies were not unusual. Slightly less than half the families had six to ten plus children. I am from one of those lucky families as I have nine brothers and one sister. Names for ten or more children requires some thought, unless you just give them numbers like No. 1, No. 2, No. 3, etc. We didn't get numbers, but someone would hang a nickname on you anyway. Even numbers would lose their importance after a nickname was given. Dad was famous for giving people nicknames. Some nicknames were clever and a match; others were off the wall and not a fit for the person with a trumped up nickname. Quite a few people in Moatsville, Clemtown, Arden, Philippi, and Tucker and Barbour Counties were known by their nicknames. If they were addressed by their given or surnames, half the people in the area wouldn't know who you were talking about. Some examples of nicknames back then included, Jackknife, Hobe, Shinney, Dingbat, Skinny Minnie, Sanky, Boots, Pood, Squibb, Railhead, Sampy, Spirit, Moofus and Bologna. I could fill the page with more colorful nicknames, but better not. Folks in Barbour County already recognize the nicknames above. More colorful names might create a problem and who needs more problems?

"What's My Name Anyway?" is a true story. It is unique, but probably not unusual for others living in the Alleghenies during the pre and post depression years.

Now, let's move on to the story.

As I mentioned earlier, I was fortunate to be a member of a large family. We also had relatives who would visit and add more kids and adults to the mix. It was not unusual for relatives to spend a weekend or more with us. Bless Mom's heart, she cooked and cleaned for and after "Cox's Army", her term for a group of relatives, and managed to be cheerful. I would have been nuts! I have problems managing multiple generations and lots of rambunctious kids. About two hours of that and I am ready to throw everybody out. She could handle it quite well. Bless my dear Mom.

On one occasion in particular, Uncle Chick, Aunt Treva, their three sons and one daughter were down from Ohio for a visit; the usual 2-4 days with us, then on to the next relative. One of Uncle Chick's treats for us was a watermelon. He and the older boys went to Philippi to shop for a melon, etc. They soon returned and he placed the melon in a wash tub with well water for cooling. Electricity had not arrived for us just yet. The evening came, supper was served, and the melon was coming up next. I was like all the other youngsters, just couldn't wait for the melon! As the table was being cleared and the knife being readied for the slicing, Mom called me aside and said, "Wib, come with me to the bedroom to try on clothes your Uncle Chick bought for you". I followed her into the bedroom. I asked her if he bought clothes for anyone else. She said, "No, only for you". The next question was, "Why me and no one else?" She paused a moment and said, "Because you are named after him." I was certain I already had a name. After all, I always responded to "Wib" when anyone spoke to me and I hadn't thought about anyone calling me "Chick". That was puzzling. I then asked, "Well, what's my name anyway"? Mom said, "It's Wilbert". I was six years old at that time and had never heard this name before. I was not too receptive to "Wilbert", but felt better with "Wilbert" than with "Chick". Wouldn't you?

I later found out that "Chick" translated to "Wilbert" and that brother Hayward at two years old couldn't say "Wilbert" and called me "Wib". Thanks, Hayward, for the nickname. It stuck with me until I entered the Army at age eighteen. I then changed my name to "Will".

What's my name anyway? I'm still working on it and considering "Wilberville". It just seems more sophisticated to me and may even represent the mother country better.

A Broken Nose
and Other Therapeutic Blows

When children have fields and meadows, rivers, streams, woods and rock ledges, snow, ice, barns and buildings as their playground, eventually an injury will occur. I had my share and do not believe I was the only one in those mountains to learn about gravity by falling out of trees. If we had had a <u>Tree</u> <u>Fallers</u> <u>Club</u>, the Club would have had a number of experienced tree fallers. Jimmy H. and I would have been Charter Members. Both of us fell from apple trees by going after <u>that</u> apple just out of reach. During lunch time at The Academy, we ventured down to Dave Findleys' place. We had spotted a crab apple tree, along a new barbed wire fence, that was ready for picking. Remember, we were scavengers and lived off the land during our noon time adventures. About five boys arrived at the tree and began selecting their apples. Most apples selected were reasonably easy to collect. Jimmy H. was after an apple higher up and proceeded to climb the tree. As bad luck would have it, he fell out while stretching for the apple. He fell beside the new barbed wired fence spread eagle. His right arm pit hit the top strand of wire on the way down. We helped him up and investigated. His arm pit had caught the barbs and they had torn a horrible gash. The wound was deep. It had opened up and torn a corner tear; two tears at a ninety degree angle with the corner making a flap. The tears were about two inches long each way. Jimmy H. bled profusely for a while. We made our way back to The Academy and explained the situation to our teacher, John S. He pulled out the first aid kit and doctored the wounds. Jimmy got lots of sympathy for a day or so. He did not, however, retrieve the prized apple. I guess the lesson learned – be careful what you reach for, especially if it's out of reach!

I should have taken notes and known about being careful. In other words, know what you are reaching for, but I didn't. On the Annon farm, our place, there were several apple trees. Some close to the house, others in orchards that Henry Annon had planted thirty to forty years earlier. The apple trees closer to home ripened early; those in the orchards a little later. Cecil and I had watched apples in the lane ripen. They were good pick and eat apples. The apple trees back then were standard apple trees and much larger than today's trees. We climbed and selected. Of course, the apple you want is at a real stretch! I was standing on a small branch near the trunk of the tree and Cecil was above me collecting his prize apple. I was about twelve years old and Cecil was ten. I had been standing on that limb for quite some time admiring "that apple" and savoring the thought of eating that little "darling". When I reached out for it, the branch under me snapped off at the trunk of the tree. I fell about twelve feet and hit the ground square on my rear. It knocked the breath out of me, but luckily I didn't break anything. I rolled in the grass gasping for some air to breathe. By the time I recovered, which seemed like f-o-r-e-v-e-r, Cecil was on the ground consoling me. I never ate that apple.

I still didn't quite understand the gravity thing as I had several falls afterwards. One fall in particular, I do believe, could have killed anyone on any given day. I believe in divine intervention and also believe it had to be operative on that particular day.

Cecil, Hayward and I were tree climbers; no different than other youngsters in our family or other families. We knew where every bird nest was within a thousand yards of our house and beyond. We had spotted a Robin's nest in a cherry tree below the house. We watched the nest being built, investigated the egg laying process and eventually saw the hatched fuzzy babies. We'd climb the tree and stand on a large limb to see the bird family; we were experienced climbers and observers. The limb we always walked out on to observe was about ten to twelve feet above a rocky area. Some of the stones were large pieces of sand stone that were discarded when Grandfather Henry built the Cellar house. Of course in West Virginia everything slopes or just drops off suddenly. That particular area sloped gradually. On that morning we were making our inspection rounds starting with the Robins in the cherry tree. We didn't carry clip boards and pens for notations on the baby Robins' progress, we just made mental notes and compared. Cecil and I were walking out the limb for the observation; plenty of smaller limbs were above us to hold onto so we didn't lose our balance. The nest was about four feet over and made it easy to see the babies. I decided I needed a closer inspection so I leaned over and grabbed a two inch limb above my head. I didn't look at the limb, just grabbed it. The limb was rotten and snapped off immediately. I went down head first, arms and limbs in a Tarzan dive; only problem, there was no water to break the fall. My belly hit a large rock before my head hit a fist size rock below. I don't remember the next few minutes, but when I did regain consciousness I was crawling toward the house. Cecil was out of the tree and had brought Mom to my rescue. She, of course, examined, mothered and treated my wounds. Divine intervention, yes; I was still alive! Since that particular fall, I have maintained a great respect for gravity.

I've discussed this experience with my adult children and said, "No telling how bright I'd have been if I had not made that Tarzan dive into a pile of rocks!" BRILLIANT! I still wear the scar from that fall. I also received a fractured skull from that fall and to this day, I have regular headaches. I definitely don't recommend Tarzan dives without eight feet of water below.

Overall, I think my brothers and sister Betty were fortunate to not have more broken bones, cuts, or severe injuries. We pushed the limits with tree acrobatics and grape vines. We used plow horses for races when the parents were visiting neighbors and swam in the creeks and rivers any chance we had. We usually came away from these events unscathed.

During a warm spring day in April of 1939, I was not so lucky. I was five years old and was in and out of the house most of the day; mostly in the house or on the porch. At that time there were no screen doors to slam. The kitchen door was open to air out the house and gave me free rein for going in and coming out. Like most five year olds, I didn't walk, I ran back and forth. It was wash day and Mom was washing clothes in a galvanized tub with a wash board and then hanging them outside on a clothes line. Some clothes were hung on a clothes line on the porch as well. She and I had made several trips in and out of the open door that day. I was playing with a little metal car; probably running the Indy 500 on two tracks, one on the porch and one in the kitchen. About 3:30 in the afternoon, I looked out the kitchen window and saw Betty and the brothers coming home from The Huffman Academy. I bolted for the open kitchen door, only it wasn't open.

Mom had closed it. My nose centered up on the door knob and the impact knocked me flat on my back on the kitchen floor. I saw two or three galaxies of stars and a half dozen Milkyways. I didn't realize there could be that many! It hurt and I was bleeding profusely. Who put that damn door knob there anyway? It wasn't there before. That was my <u>first</u> broken nose. Of course the connection between my nose and a stationary door knob stopped the Indy 500 race. I couldn't see to finish the race and was being attended to by Mom, the track physician. She picked me up, sat me near the wash basin and washed my face. She pulled my nose to see if it was broken and it was. Thank God she didn't yank on it to set it! After most of the bleeding stopped, she stuffed my nose with cotton, patted me on the head and said, "You'll be okay". That was comforting, but my nose hurt anyway. I did get further attention when The Academy bunch arrived home. The brothers asked, "What in the hell has he done this time"? Betty was more kind; she asked me what happened and then took me to the living room, sitting down with me in a rocking chair. I sat on Betty's lap and explained how the door knob jumped in front of my nose. Of course, I was dramatic in retelling how that happened; more attention and sympathy from her was worth the acting and reliving the event. The brothers didn't want to hear about it. They said "come show us"! I wasn't about to center up on that door knob again.

I have had six broken noses since then. All of them occurred while playing basketball. Three of those required surgery and straightening. The brothers and Betty now say, "Do you think he will ever learn"? There isn't a lot of bone left in the Proboscis! Maybe I should retire my Jersey!

85

A Sod Sandwich
and Other Pranks at the Academy

A Sod Sandwich

The Huffman Academy was a place of learning both indoors and out. My experience there from 1941 to 1949 was pleasant and rewarding. Today I feel the same and wouldn't trade that experience with anyone I have ever known. Teachers were special people and our leaders. We respected them and held them in high regard. Other kids in The Academy soon became our school family and social contacts outside the home. We learned to cooperate, pay attention, act responsibly, and help one another. Older students often acted as tutors for younger kids, assisted the teacher by teaching reading or math sessions for the lower grades, and always included any and all kids in games at recess or lunch break. Sound idyllic? It was.

We did, however, cross the boundaries a time or two. I expect most young people test the limits from time to time. Even in the best of situations someone steps over the line. As a cousin has said, "maybe we shouldn't discuss this". "I still live here and I don't want the locals to know." Protect the reputation if possible was the message. We discussed some of the following anyway.

One spring day after a rain, probably mid-April, cousin Bill, brother Hayward and I finished our lunch quickly and went outside. We were the first three out; cousin Bill was a tad older, Hayward was a fifth grader, and I was in the third grade. The ground was soggy wet with lush green grass in the fence row. Cousin Bill said, "Let's throw a tuft of sod through the transom and stir things up!" The transom above the door was open so we had a clear shot. We'd throw the tuft of sod and hide behind the coal house; that was the plan. We reached down, grabbed a handful of grass and pulled it up; roots, grass, and wet dirt. On the count of three, we'd throw it through the transom. One, two, three, and throw! We did it! One of the soggy missiles went through. Two hit near the opening with grass and soggy soil sliding down the door. We had no idea what happened inside. As we ducked behind the coal house, we heard all kinds of chatter and shuffling as the other students exited the building; some were laughing, some were talking and wondering who the culprits were. Talk about stirring up a hornets' nest! We did! As everyone exited and mingled, the three of us, one at a time, joined them trying to stay "undercover". We didn't think much about the fact that it's hard to stay undercover in such a small population of only 20 kids. We were lucky that the teacher, Doc, did not come out immediately; reason being, the sod had traveled through the transom and hit him square in the mouth while eating his egg sandwich. He and others were totally surprised and stunned by the direct hit. By the time he cleaned the dirt sandwich out of his mouth, all the students were outside. He would never know which student(s) had fired the sod missile unless someone who did know snitched on us. To my knowledge, no one ever did. The Academy's family rules held tight; don't tattle. Cousin Bill, Hayward and I were model students for a week or so after that. We waited for a few weeks hoping no one would blow the whistle on us. They didn't. We were free at last, free at last!

<u>School Bells and Whistles</u>

Most teachers called the students in after recess or lunch break with a whistle or hand held bell. They would slip out on the porch and blow the whistle or ring the bell. At The Huffman Academy it was usually a whistle. The whistle was preferred because we could hear it half a mile away. We roamed pretty far out. What freedom! Students today never leave the school yard. I am thankful every day that we weren't stuck in the boundaries of a school yard. I would rather be like the free range chickens and explore.

One of the tricks the boys at The Academy pulled on Mr. H was to stay behind the school house and not come in when he blew the whistle. We would wait until he stepped off the porch. He would blow the whistle again and come looking for us. We could look through the cracks in the dry stacked rock foundation wall and see his legs. If he started around the upper side we would go to the lower side and stay one side ahead of him, looking and watching for him to continue or switch back. Usually he would make one trip around the school and come in. Most of the time we would do one round and sneak in the school house and be "studying" when he entered the building. Mr. H, for some reason, never reprimanded us or knew exactly who had led him on the chase. We didn't do this often, but when we felt a need to trick Mr. H, we would pull this stunt again.

On some occasions, if he did a switch back on us, we would take him around the school house two to four times before we sneaked back in. I have wondered since then, who was tricking whom?

Mr. H was the most gentle and laid back teacher I had at The Academy. I had a very strict and disciplinary teacher in the sixth grade, Mr. C. He kept a tight rein on all of us. Mr. C walked tall and was all business. He would easily fit the image of a headmaster. I respected all of my teachers. I mention the different styles of these two teachers and must say I learned equally from both ends of the spectrum.

I attended sixth grade at The Moatsville Academy under Mr. Cornwell. He kept us pretty close to the school. The only activity off school property was softball and basketball about a thousand yards up Glade Run. Mr. Ritter gave us permission to set up a softball diamond and a basketball backboard. We had many challenging games in that field; no fights or broken noses, just competitive games.

"Thuck"

I recall one little incident that I pulled at The Moatsville Academy that upset my teacher, Mr. Cornwell. Mr. C always had us sing a little prayer song before we ate our lunch. We would sing the song and have a resounding AMEN at the end. The older boys liked that part and would use their new found bass voices to hammer the AMEN, putting an exclamation point after the song. Most days we were in a respectful and prayerful mood; after all, we were hungry and couldn't wait to grab our lunch bags and gulp down a ham or peanut butter sandwich. I had been at The Moatsville Academy about seven months and had participated in spelling bees, Christmas plays, been a janitor, played on the school softball team and had a good relationship with Mr. C. My seat was next to the last one in the row of seats on the cloak room side; easy access to the lunch bags, boots, coats, etc. Older students sat in the rear while younger students sat up front. Seats were sized to fit the students; small seats in the front of the row with seats getting larger and larger until the last seat row in the back of the room. I do not recall the number of students in attendance there, but my best guess is twenty four. There were four other boys in sixth grade with me; Danny, Lloyd, John and Billy. We sat in that order. We were singing the lunchtime prayer song one day and for some reason after the resounding AMEN, I added "thuck" loud and clear. For those who do not understand "thuck", it's the noise a chicken makes when it gets a kernel of corn stuck in its throat. "Thuck"!

That "thuck" filled a quiet prayerful atmosphere like a clap of thunder. Mr. C quickly jumped up from his desk and headed our way. He was angry and it showed. Someone had not only violated his rule, but that "thuck" was blasphemous; a major, major error in judgment and someone was destined to be punished. All students sat quietly and watched as Mr. C approached our corner of the room with whipping stick in hand. I was as guilty as a snake, but managed to keep my composure. I was pretty good at holding my composure, because my tail had been in trouble a few times before. Mr. C grabbed John, yanked him out of his seat and had the whipping stick raised over his shoulder ready to let the "thuck" kid take his due punishment. Cuz John quickly said, "Wasn't me, Mr. C, wasn't me!" Mr. C regained his composure and realized he had the wrong "thuck" kid. I am thankful he didn't know who it was and that he returned to his desk in front of the room. I was also thankful and proud of Cuz John for not squealing on me. The students were pretty quiet during the remainder of the lunch period. They resumed the laughter and louder play outside.

It didn't occur to me why Mr. C was so angry over "thuck" until years later. I think he heard the "F" word and that sent him over the edge; can't blame him for that. I have mentioned before that we didn't tattle. It was an honor code thing; not written, but understood. If someone broke the unwritten, unspoken honor code, all of us would be in trouble. We didn't and cousin John didn't. Thanks John!

Survival Skills Early On and Cecil's Revenge

In large families you learn to become independent and fend for yourself early on. It's almost like "root hog or die". You also learn not to go for the last piece of chicken if you don't want a fork in the back of your hand. I really feel badly about the following incident; however, it describes the learning curve and survival skills early in life.

I do not remember this incident or perhaps have just chosen to block it from my memory vault. I'm not sure which; maybe it's both. I was about two years old and the "baby", Cecil, was about six months old. Aah huh... memory returns as I write. That little rascal replaced me, dethroned me, and kicked me out of my comfort zone as "the baby". I had to retaliate! I'd best tone it down or I may re-experience the hurt of dethronement again. Maybe wounds don't heal; just scab over and wait for decapitation later on. I think the scab just got lifted after seventy four years. Wow, that's incredible. Snap out of it Will and get back to the story!

As I previously mentioned, I was about two and Cecil was around six months of age. Mom was a really good mother; very protective and always guarding over her flock. Cecil was the youngest of nine children, ages ranging from twelve to the "baby" (Cecil). Mom was wise to all tricks and manipulative behaviors within her flock. If something didn't look right, she intuitively knew it and went about correcting it immediately.

At two years old, I was about to be discovered just like when Hollywood stars are discovered; picked from the crowd, because they stand out. You know they're special. Well, sometimes being special ain't so good. Mom noticed the "baby" was getting slimmer and slimmer. "What's happening to my "baby"? Cecil hadn't started solid food yet, but close to it. Her radar had also picked up that a two year old was hitting an early growth spurt. He (me) was a healthy "dethroned baby"; always active, large for his age and getting larger, possibly sporting a "milk gut". Mom decided she'd investigate, maybe do some undercover work to determine why the 'baby" was starving to death while the two year old was growing like he's on a "milk and honey diet".

Her undercover work paid off. She gave us both our bottles with Cecil in the crib and me under it with my feet sticking up in the springs. Mom left the room, but came back close enough for her undercover work and watched us from the other room. She was amazed to see a precious two year old guzzle his bottle down, get up, and switch the empty bottle for the full one the "baby" was leisurely drawing down. She watched as I made the switch and returned to my dethroned spot under the crib. I don't remember any harsh words, but I certainly remember a change in the bottle feeding regimen. I was quickly placed on solid food and drank milk from a small glass after being "discovered". A glass of milk just wasn't ever the same. I do not and have not drunk milk from a glass in seven decades. I do not like milk as a drink; go figure.

Cecil, the "baby", survived the starvation plan that the dethroned two year old had in place, thanks to a mother who loved her flock. I think she was able to love me still. Cecil, sorry I took your milk!

Cecil's Revenge

Cecil and I were enrolled at The Moatsville Academy from 1946 to 1947; he in fourth grade and I in the sixth. It was easy to make the transition from The Huffman Academy to The Moatsville Academy. It was the same distance; about a mile. The Moatsville Academy was located on our road in downtown Moatsville. Moatsville at that time had three churches, two stores, a post office, eighteen homes, over sixty people, forty dogs, ninety cats (they multiply fast), and two creeks. However, there were no grapevines to swing on going to or coming from school. That was the most difficult adjustment. No grapevines? Really?

Nevertheless, Cecil, I and the Ritter and Price kids did find other excitement and recreation there. We played lots of stick ball, splashed in Glade Run, and got into making "bottle bombs". Dry carbide in a bottle with a little water added to it produces gas. We'd place the carbide and water in a bottle, screw the lid on, throw it in Glade Run and watch it float down stream. Sooner or later it would explode, leaving bottle shards and small pieces of glass in the creek. We were extremely lucky that no one lost an eye or hand. We did recognize danger when loading the carbide and water. We screwed the cap on quickly and lobbed it in rushing water, never still water. We never used the "bottle bomb" near the school where little kids were. We were ahead of the "pipe bomb" curve. No one got arrested or hurt at The

Academy and not a single "bomb maker" went to prison or any further into pyrotechnics. Too dangerous!

Back to Cecil's revenge. Cecil, I and five other Academy students were walking down our road toward home. As we arrived at their cut off or home, Cecil and I would continue to walk. One fine fall afternoon, he and I harvested a couple of apples from Fred's hog lot. After all, we, the other kids, and hogs had been harvesting those apples for a spell. That day for some reason we were separated from the other students. We wanted an apple so we climbed over the fence and checked out the apples still hanging on the tree. The hogs had feasted on any apples that had fallen and there were very few left on the tree due to seven kids passing and harvesting apples every day after school. Any remaining apples were up high in the tree so there was no standing and picking – that phase of the harvest had passed along with the long stick harvest phase.

Now harvesting was reduced to stoning the apples out of the tree. We selected carefully; Cecil's eye on his apple, my eye on mine. Throwing size rocks were plentiful so we just picked and threw. I missed the first throw, but hit with the second while Cecil was still lobbing rocks. The hogs moved to the far side of the pen. Of course, we may have encouraged that a bit. We didn't want to get in a wrestling match with dirty hogs over fallen apples. A couple of small rocks in the hogs' direction encouraged them to advance to the rear side of the pen and stay there. I retrieved my apple and was helping Cecil with his apple harvest. I launched a nice stone. It hit a limb and returned to hit Cecil in the head. It was a pretty good throw for a third baseman I thought, but I didn't want it to return and hit Cecil. I'd rather the squashed apple return. In any event, he recovered with only a trickle of blood, no mortal wound, and I wouldn't have to carry or assist him up the mountain. We finally knocked "his apple" down and retrieved it. The hogs remained in their safe zone until we were out of sight. For all I know, they may still be leaning against that fence shaking.

Cecil and I enjoyed the apples as we walked on toward home. Salt would have made them better, but we enjoyed and finished our apples anyway. I had asked Cecil a few times if his head hurt and had told him that I was sorry. I certainly didn't plan for the rock to bounce off a limb and hit him. I was good, but not that good in the throwing department. I thought he had fully accepted my concern and apology. My mind had recovered from shame and guilt.

We had finished the apples and were midway on our trek home when Cecil threw a rock from lethal range. He hadn't hit an apple all day, but his rock hit the side of my head! I saw stars for quite some time. When I could finally stand upright, he said, "I got you back". That behavior for Cecil was so far out of character I couldn't fathom his logic. Was he "getting me back" for the rock that kicked back and hit him? I had apologized and doctored his wound. What had I forgotten?

I've thought a lot about Cecil's "getting me back" statement and finally concluded that his "getting me back" that day was somehow connected to a "bottle bellied two year old" who took his bottle eleven years earlier. Remember the scab thing? On that fall day in 1946, I had lifted his scab from an eleven year old wound. Watch for old scabs and don't lift one.

Cecil -- 1941

And Then There Was David

My part in the tenth son's arrival to join the Ball Family began at four o'clock in the morning on February 2, 1942. Needless to say, waking a seven year old boy from his warm bed and happy dreams so early on a chilly moon lit morning wasn't conducive to smiling and greeting anyone warmly. I liked my sleep then and still do. My response to that now would be, take two aspirin and call me later.

At seven years old, I had not received sex education at The Huffman Academy or at home. The only sex education received was observing the bull and girl cow in the fields doing their happy dance or seeing the old rooster work his harem of hot chicks. If we asked, "where do babies come from", the standard answer was "under a rock". Well, I can't begin to recall the number of rocks I turned over the previous two years looking for a baby, but I had not found any up to that point.

Mom dispatched brother Hayward and me to Grandma Nestor's house with a note for Aunt Eva. Hayward was in charge of the note and also aware of its contents. After all, he was nine years old and knew about babies on their way. He just held the note and said "come on". I don't remember him rebelling or using any church words during our one mile journey on that cold February morning. I, on the other hand, used all the church words I had learned in church and made up a few more. In other words, I cussed all the way to Grandma's. Why in the hell are we going to school at this time in the morning? Well, it went downhill from there. I still did not know what was about to unfold.

I'm guessing the note from Mom was asking Aunt Eva to come quickly; the baby is on the way. Would I have been any happier if I'd been privy to this important information? I'm really not sure. It was still four o'clock in the morning, very cold, and I was walking one mile through a moon lit morning.

We waited at Grandma's until eight o'clock that morning and then finished the trip to The Huffman Academy. The Huffman Academy was a one room school with one teacher and twelve to twenty students from first through eighth grades. In retrospect, it was a wonderful place to grow and learn. I'll elaborate more on The Huffman Academy later on.

Once at school, I settled in for the day, calmed down, did the usual 3 R's, enjoyed recess and lunch break and began the long journey home. I still did not know. Looking back, I think Hayward was practicing his obligation and respect for confidentiality. He held that information like a skunk in a steel trap. Not a peep, just a zipped lip. We took the lower trail back home that afternoon and followed the Glade Run Road. As we were passing the first house on the right, Dave Findley's two story house, we spotted Dave working in the yard. I think he spent two hours or more there just waiting to share the news. News traveled fast in that end of Barbour County. There were no telephones, few automobiles, and for some reason horseback was not used much. Horses eat lots of hay and that was expensive; therefore, if you were going to feed <u>anything</u> you expected it to work, not be used for pleasure.

Back to Dave Findley and his news. "Hey, Ball boys, I hear you have a new brother on the hill." I said something to the effect, "(expletive) I don't believe that." He insisted, "Yes, it's true." Hayward didn't help Dave F with the news. Remember his confidentiality standards? I mumbled a few not so nice words and walked on with brother Hayward, Edith, John, and Shirley. We left the Glade Run Road and cut through Uncle Short's property (John's father) and the Holmes' farm and finally topped out on our farm. We were still a quarter mile from the house when I noticed that Hayward had picked up the pace; I followed his lead.

We finally arrived home, stepped inside and you guessed it! There in a bed was Mom and a little red and blue, black haired, closed eye boy. It was "Bro David". I was stunned! How could they find this baby when I had turned over all the bigger rocks on the farm? How was it possible to have missed the David Rock?

I have since discussed my reactions to these events with Bro David and he assured me he didn't hear a single cuss word that day. It was an event that a seven year old boy never forgets and most of all, it was worth every step and cuss word I could think of that day. Another brother! David Lynn.

<u>Reflection</u>. As I recall this event, place, time, and characters involved, I'm reminded of a happy and full day. I am also snapped back to the reality that ninety percent of the characters mentioned here are gone;

nothing left but dust and fragile cobwebs in my mind. I see the dust particles and fragile cobwebs float by and I cry. I yearn for only a touch, a thought, a greeting or a conversation. The touch, thought, greeting and conversation does occur, but in reality it is only one sided. It springs from within me as I quietly listen and remember.

Funerals

Funerals are funerals. The deceased person's life is celebrated in a somber to joyful ceremony. Joyful to somber is dictated by the family of the deceased. Usually it is not a pleasant experience. Friends, family and the attending personnel (minister, undertaker, military or other organizations) are present to show respect for the deceased and family. It is an emotional time for all in that the departed has left us and it reminds us that it could have been one of us.

Funerals today are much different in that the Funeral Home staff and the deceased's family arrange the funeral from beginning to end. The deceased no longer goes back to the family home which was the custom a few decades ago. I was six years old when my brother Charles died. He was almost two years old. His body was brought back home and placed in one of the bedrooms. At six years old I watched the emotional state of six brothers, one sister and my parents as they struggled with the loss. It was very confusing to me, because I had never witnessed such a loss. I wasn't tearful until neighbors and friends came by and the family (Mom especially) would break down and cry again when they went in the room to see the baby lying in a tiny coffin. The funeral came and went, but seemed like forever to me. I couldn't get my feelings figured out. I wasn't sure if I should play, smile, laugh, or be obnoxious, angry or loving. It was not easy for a six year old boy. Little kids were to be seen and not heard. I don't remember any comforting words other than, "eventually, it will be alright". What's eventually mean anyway? All events during Charles' funeral were a blur. Somehow the family managed with all the visitors, extended family and friends and soon pulled together to recover. It wasn't pleasant, but they did it. Often, families who had lost young children were exceptionally helpful and visited frequently. Their presence made a difference in the recovery process.

Years later I was asked to help with a funeral. I didn't and still don't like funerals. I accept death and funerals as a part of life; however, that doesn't mean I have to like it. I was about fourteen years old before I had a better grasp of the meaning of death. Someone asked me to help haul Uncle Short from the Ritter Place up to the England Graveyard; haul as in hauling the body to the gravesite on a sled with a team of horses. It was wintertime and a hearse could not make it up there. The trip was up a rocky and rutted out road. A four wheel drive Hummer might have made it, but nothing else except a team and a sled. I'm sure I wasn't the only person to haul a corpse to a graveyard in the Alleghenies. Quite a few graveyards were on mountain top farms with access roads only for funerals. The England graveyard was on top of the Auvil Farm. I think those Mountaineers liked being on top and closer to God.

In any event, I was the designated driver. Neither I nor the horses were too happy about having a dead person riding on the sled one half mile to the grave site. The horses were "skittish" and kept looking at me and then back at the coffin on the sled. I walked beside the most spirited horse and talked to her as we made our way through the slush, ice, and snow. I was fourteen years old and familiar with handling a team of horses. Finally, we made it to the grave site and without losing the load.

The attendants at the gravesite untied the ropes, holding the coffin in place. They carried the coffin to the grave, placed it on supports over the grave, and waited. No one said "Thank you" or offered any payment. They just recommended that I take the team and go home. My mission was accomplished so that is what I did. As I retraced the steps back toward the Ritter Place, I passed the funeral procession walking up to the cemetery. It was a somber procession and the horses didn't like it. They acted like they wanted to get out of "Dodge" and we did. I went home and un-harnessed them, fed them and turned them loose. As I was doing this, we (the horses and I) could see and hear singing at the graveyard ceremony. The horses perked up their ears and listened. The gravesite was on the same mountain as our farm, but lower in elevation. It was about a half mile away and one bench down from the top of our mountain. Neither I nor the horses were very happy about being drafted for funeral duty. It might have been helpful if someone would have discussed the process beforehand and asked afterwards if I was okay, but they didn't.

My guess is that this was the Mountaineer way. You have a job to do, you do it, no questions asked. What's next? Allegheny folks were not into discussing their feelings and were not equipped to help me sort out my feelings about hauling Uncle Short to his resting place on top of the Auvil Farm. They were more into the task at hand; finish it and then head home for supper.

I still don't like funerals and that experience at an early age didn't help. I must add that Uncle Short was one of my favorite uncles. He and his family visited often. He and Dad worked for the B&O Railroad on the same Track Maintenance Crew. Dad had several work related stories to share about "Shorty". I can see "Shorty" right now, wringing his clasped hands as he unwinds a story to one of his old railroad buddies. God speed "Shorty".

Stilts and Eating Sod

Spring time in the Alleghenies was a time of renewal. A busy time filled with hustle and bustle activities, such as preparing fields and gardens for planting, cleaning, and picking up inside and outside; these were the usual spring rituals. I think "spiffing" up the premises was prompted by trying to stay up with spring flowers, plants and greening of the grass. Everything looks clean and lush after a dull and drab winter. New excitement and energy for spring time seemed like a spiritual renewal as well.

Mom and Betty always did spring cleaning. It took about a week, because they did lots of washing and scrubbing. We learned to stay clear of the house for two main reasons. Number one, if you were in the house, you immediately got drafted for the cleaning detail. Number two, if you stood still too long, you would get scrubbed or washed as well. Doors were left open to air out the house. Walls and windows were scrubbed and lots of stuff discarded. Discarded here means removed from the house and stored in the smoke house. Nothing was really discarded, just reassigned to a different place or used for some other purpose. I've explained to my adult children that on the farm if you didn't get at least three uses from an item, something was wrong. They are catching on to this, I think.

About every fourth year during purging and cleaning, Mom would purchase linoleum for the kitchen; a twelve by eighteen foot piece. She and Betty would cut and lay it to fit. Here's the good part for a nine year old boy. The linoleum was shipped in a twelve foot cardboard cylinder; two six foot pieces taped together in the middle. I couldn't wait to experiment with the two six foot cylinders.

I had seen pictures of circus clowns walking on high stilts and had experienced walking on stilts we had made from small trees. Our stilts were usually made so your feet were two to three feet above ground; not six to eight like the clowns. The six foot cylinders were a good height and the hole was big enough for sticking your feet in it.

I asked Mom for the cylinders. None of the other brothers, younger or older, seemed interested. Did they know something that I didn't? If they did, they didn't offer any information. My plan was to climb up on a low shed roof, insert my feet, pull the cylinders up until they stopped at the groin area, push off and walk around in the half acre chicken/wood lot. Getting them on was easy and a good snug fit; a "piece of cake", I thought. I had not at that time, however, had pilot training, as in a pilot taking off being the easy part. It takes more training and practice to land. I had not thought about the landing part. All I was going to do was push off, walk around the chicken/wood lot until I had attracted an audience, show off a little, return to the launching area, set down on the roof and remove the cylinder type stilts. I'm not sure if anyone was watching or not, but I was ready for the maiden walk!

I pushed off and took two stumbling steps and began to fall forward. I had not done the experimental test; hold onto the building to see if one could actually walk. I found out the hard way that if you can't bend your knees, or lift the cylinder off the ground for the next step, you are in trouble. My two steps did get me clear of the building and a chopping block, but the fall was stiff and uncoordinated and I fell like a tree. My face, nose, and chin hit the soft moist sod pretty hard. I came up off the ground with a well fertilized (chicken shit) mouth full of sod. That stuff did not taste good! I rolled around in the grass and other stuff trying to push the cylinders off before a crowd of spectators gathered. I was lucky they hadn't and no one called me the "stilt man" or worse, "sod eater", or even worse, "chicken shit eater".

I learned something that day concerning experimental trials. Always think it through and don't let enthusiasm get ahead of logic. What if?

Walking and Riding

During the 1940's my family did not own a car. If we went to visit or go to the store at the bottom of the mountain, we walked. No one ever complained; it was just a way of life. There were three vehicles on our road and twelve houses. That averaged out to twenty-five percent of the residents on our road owned vehicles. My guess is that this statistic was the average for other communities in the Alleghenies. If you rode any place in a car, it was appreciated and a joyous occasion. If someone stopped and offered a ride, it was accepted and at the drop off point the driver was sincerely thanked. Most folks knew one another and if you, as a youngster, didn't know the driver, they knew your family. Safety was not a big issue back then. Unfortunately, times have changed for the worse in this department. Today I'd cringe if one of my children accepted a ride with someone they didn't know.

The following two stories stand out in my mind as opposite ends of the ride spectrum. The first ride was during the late winter months of 1945. Our teacher at The Academy offered six of us a ride down Glade Run Road. There was snow on the ground and ice covered the dirt road. It was one of those sunshiny cold days with water on top of the ice in places where it puddled up. The six of us, John, Shirley, Edith, Hayward, Cecil, and I piled in Doc's (our teacher) car and off we went down Glade Run Road. Doc dropped us off at

John and Shirley's driveway. We would cut through their farm, the Holmes' Farm, and then head up to our places. Doc stopped and we piled out, said thank you and goodbye. In front of the drop off spot was a small rise in the road. For some reason we four boys decided to try to hold the car back. We ditched books and dinner pails and grabbed the rear bumper. Doc let out the clutch and started moving. We were holding and sliding on the wet icy road. When the car started up the small incline it started spinning and we held on; man against machine. We held the car as it was spinning and throwing slush back on us. Further up the incline the car began to slide toward a deep ditch on the upper side of the road. We held on, it slid and wound up in the ditch, stuck. Doc would gun it forward and back. Finally, he put it in neutral and got out. It was about 3:30 in the afternoon, he was stuck and it would be dark soon. He was in a pickle and needed help! Of course we offered help. He had us push forward as hard as we could while he gunned it. The car just dug deeper and spun the wheels. He soon realized he needed more than four boys to get him out of the ditch. After some discussion, cousin John said, "Queenie can do it, Queenie can do it." Queenie was their horse. We left Doc and went with John to get Queenie and one of his older brothers to pull the car out. Hayward, Cecil, Edith and I then left the scene and went home. We had confidence that "Queenie could do it."

The next day John told us about how he, his brother, and Queenie pulled the car from the ditch. Doc was grateful for the help and gave John and his brother each a dollar for their help. It was not uncommon for people to get stuck, ditched, or have a breakdown on those country roads during the winter time. If that happened, the nearest farmer would help pull the vehicle out. I pulled a cream truck out of a ditch below our house once and received four dollars, two dollars for me and a dollar each for the horses. Folks in the mountains didn't rely on providing their towing services for income. A breakdown might occur once in five years, unless you could create one of course. We never bragged to the other Academy students about holding Doc's car and putting it in the ditch. He apparently didn't know either. We offered help and arranged to get his car out. What else could we do?

A second riding event occurred in 1950. Carl, my oldest brother, Hayward and I hitched a ride to Philippi to see a movie. It was one of those early spring days; chilly and rainy too. God, I hated to get wet. Brother Carl was treating me and Hayward to a movie. He was in between work and being drafted into the Korean War. We watched the movie, got out about nine o'clock that evening, and started our journey home. It had begun to rain one of those drizzles that last forever. Brother Carl knew someone and asked for a ride. We rode about three miles south on Route 250. Our Route, Route 38, cut East, North East, from that intersection. Brother Carl was wearing a suit and tie. Hayward and I were in our best jeans and plaid shirts. We stationed ourselves in a stretch of road where cars could easily pull off the road and pick us up if they chose to.

As luck would have it, one of the first cars pulled over. The driver, "Kelley", was from Moatsville, our destination. We felt lucky that someone from Moatsville had stopped. "Kelley" rolled the window down, looked us over, said hello and drove off. Brother Carl had a swear word vocabulary that topped all charts! He used every one of those swear words to unleash his feelings toward "Kelley". I think he may have repeated the list before he calmed down. It was raining harder when "Stover" picked us up and dropped us off at "Boot Jack". We had three more miles to go after that. We walked across three farm fields and one had tall wet "river grass" in it.

We finally got home about eleven thirty that night. All other family members were bedded down. When we entered the bedroom to undress and get ready for bed, Brother Carl said, "Damn it, I left here looking like a Philadelphia lawyer and came back looking like Pete, the tramp". He had calmed down considerably and chuckled at his assessment of our movie adventure. Other than getting wet and having to walk the last three miles, it was a good adventure. Plus, I learned a few more swear words.

About a week later, none other than "Kelley" showed up at the house for a visit and a free meal. We ate and sat on the porch with Dad and "Kelley". Dad asked me and Carl to play a few tunes for "Kelley". That lit Carl's fuse again! He was determined to NOT play anything for that damn "Kelley". He proceeded to break a guitar string so Dad would not continue to ask us to entertain "Kelley". Later on brother Carl told Dad about "Kelley" not picking us up. Dad said he didn't know that or he would not have asked us to play. Dad was okay with the roundabout refusal to play for "Kelley".

Years later, "Kelley's" son told us that his dad didn't pick us up because he didn't want to get his car wet. Needless to say, he (Kelley) didn't get any further favors, music, or conversation out of three of Rasty's sons. I hope Mom didn't feed him next time he came for a visit. Remember, I do not like to get wet!

112

Swimming and Spitting

Spitting on the Ritter kids' feet and getting sick on Beech Nut Chewing Tobacco or a plug of Honey Cut Tobacco wasn't fun after all.

During the long hot summer months, Mom had us well organized. She was the farm manager. I suspect all of us obtained more of our management skills from her than any college courses on Personnel Management. She led by example and wouldn't turn us loose without getting the project started. A typical day on that mountain top farm in Barbour County would go something like this: up at 6:30 in the morning, have breakfast, which usually consisted of fried potatoes, baked biscuits, ham or sausage patty, gravy, two eggs, butter and jelly, and then begin doing the daily chores: milk the cows, feed livestock, chop wood and bring in coal to heat the cook stove as needed and of course, draw water from the well for the day's use. Normally, we were in the fields early and working by 8:00 in the morning, whether it was cultivating with a horse and cultivator, mowing, or putting in and up hay (let me explain in and up). We put hay in the small barn loft and what wouldn't go there had to be stacked (put up). We worked until 12:00 noon and then had dinner (city folk call this lunch). I still like the dinner and supper terms. At 1:00 in the afternoon we were back at work until whatever lasted to 5:00 o'clock. Supper came after we took care of the tools and fed the horse, usually about 5:30 in the evening. After supper, we had evening chores, such as feeding and watering livestock, chopping kindling and bringing in coal for the next day (that was my chore). I didn't do well with the milking skill, plus I didn't like being slapped in the face with a dirty tail. It not only hurt, but you never knew what was tangled in that thing.

After the chores were done, supper was over, and we had made our plans for the next day, we were free for the rest of the evening. Here's where the swimming and spitting comes in.

Of course after a hot day in the fields we were tired and dirty, but always had the energy to walk to Moatsville and up Teters Creek to the Moore Hole. That was about one and one half miles from home. A mountain stream is always refreshing after being in the hot sun most of the day. The Moore Hole was a wonderful place for young boys. Occasionally a girl or two would go, but they would be accompanied by family – wise choice.

The Hole wasn't anything close to an Olympic swimming pool. Its greatest feature was a huge boulder right smack dab in the middle of Teter Creek. Its lower side was about 6' above water while the top and middle sides of the boulder were about 20 feet high. Needless to say, the high end got more activity. There were two reasons for this; one, the water was deeper there; about 6' deep and about 10' wide. The second and more important reason was this got more attention; you could jump or dive and generally show off your acrobatics here. A few youngsters developed their jumping and diving skills there. Tragically, one poor diver broke his back there as well.

After a hard day's work and about an hour or so of swimming we were re-energized. We had to be, because we had a one and a half mile walk back to our mountain top farm. That's the swimming part. The spitting part is on its way.

Galls Store in Moatsville was about half a mile from the Moore Hole. We'd usually stop there for a RC Cola (16 oz.) and one pack of Planters peanuts, which was shared. We would pour the nuts into the RC Cola and then sit on the loading dock outside the store to enjoy it. Peanuts and the RC Cola were so refreshing and often brought tears and a burp to a ten year old boy. Aah. I don't know where the oldest brother got the money for the treat, but it was and still is appreciated. (I wonder if Mom gave them a dollar to treat us for a good day's work.)

During our refreshment stop, bro Don, on several occasions, would be in charge of refreshments. He would have enough money to treat four younger brothers and just enough left over to purchase a bag of Beechnut Chewing Tobacco or a plug of Honeycutt. I have wondered about the funds, because there wasn't any loose change anywhere around that I can remember. Maybe brother Don had the authority to put it on Dad's bill? In any event, we were refreshed and refueled to walk the remaining mile home up the mountain.

We'd get off the loading dock, stretch, and start our journey home. A few paces up our road and out of sight of the store, bro Don would give each of us a chew of tobacco (without instructions on chewing – like don't swallow this stuff!) I think he knew what he was doing and what would happen later. He was 15 or 16 years old and had experience with chewing tobacco.

The Ritter family lived about one quarter mile up our road. There were four older Ritters in this episode. Like us, they would be barefoot and they would always come out to the road as the five of us passed their place. We swam at least four of the five days per week and made such a good parade past their house.

Like most little kids, we would follow and duplicate the oldest brother's leadership. Don gave us a chew. We chewed, he'd spit to the right and we'd spit to the right. He held the tobacco juice for a long spit so we held it too. (You know what happens when you have a mouth full of juice – you swallow some.) We didn't know for lack of experience, so follow our leader we did. When we passed the Ritter house, we were loaded up with a wad of Beechnut or Honeycutt and a mouth full of spit. There on the side of the road on a hot summer evening in July 1944 we unloaded that juice on the Ritter kids' bare feet. I believe they were totally caught off guard. All they could do was dance and try to avoid a second volley. I don't recall any squalling or swearing, only dancing.

We moved on thinking nothing of the spitting episode and of course, hoping Mom or Dad Ritter would not tell Dad (Rasty Ball). If they had, I believe I wouldn't be telling this true story.

You have heard it said that we'll get our just rewards for our deeds. I'm a believer, because we did before we topped out on our mountain that day. About two thirds of the way up the mountain, Lewis, Hayward, Cecil and I started turning from pale white to green, got very dizzy and began puking our guts out. It took us twice the time to get home that evening and needless to say, no one except Don enjoyed the end of that swimming and spitting trip. I hope the Ritter boys have forgiven us.

The Academy Rules vs. Rasty's Rules

I recall there being two major types of rules; those that were spoken, written, explained, and easily understood, and those not spoken, written, explained, or easily understood until after the fact. I'll call the latter "after the fact rules".

The formula for the Academic Rules was as follows: teacher formulates the rules, explains the rules for any misbehavior, then outlines the consequences for the misbehavior. "Do you understand?" "Yes, we do", would be the reply from all students. We felt important to be informed. Know – misbehave – suffer consequences - easy and effective.

Rasty's formula for rules was almost in reverse order. Unknown rule - misbehave – suffer – know. His consequences for misbehavior came first. (His definition for misbehavior was not universal; operative words here are <u>his definition</u>.) Sometimes after the consequence he'd explain, but most often he did not. Was this confusing? Yes. Was this hurtful? Yes. This was always hurtful in two ways. Not only did you have a sore rear, but you were also left feeling confused and angry. At that particular moment a little hatred and rage stirred in your gut. This wasn't very effective when you think about the confusion part, but effective if you parent by using the <u>fear</u> dynamic. I didn't like the fear dynamics used as a parenting tool then nor would

I encourage it as a parenting tool today. Rasty's fear tool did keep ten boys in check for awhile and more importantly it gave us several years to study "mind reading". We learned to "read" Dad's mind pretty well, but never quite totally mastered it. We still had to cut our own "width" (his word for switch) occasionally. He kept the rules to himself. I think he did this to keep us off guard and in check. If we knew "his rules" we'd figure out how to get around them and it would have totally destroyed his control over us. Here's an example of his formula.

One hot Sunday afternoon in July 1942, we had some neighbors (the Prices) in for dinner and an afternoon visit. There were three Price kids and a couple other neighborhood kids playing stick ball with us in the cow pasture. At about two o'clock we took a water break. Water was drawn from a well on the porch back then. A long slim well bucket was dropped down the well, filled and drawn up by a windlass (crank handle). We were sweaty and thirsty and lined up to take a drink from a common dipper. We were talking a bit about the game and some other things, while the adults were on the porch visiting with each other. I thought we were pretty well behaved. I was about fourth in line and talking junk about the game, I guess, when Dad took a dipper of the 56 degree water from a kid ready for her drink and threw it in my face. I didn't know then nor do I know today what prompted that from him. He spoke not a word, joined the neighbors on the porch and continued the adult conversation. I was shocked and embarrassed due to his behavior. Brother Hayward said "It wasn't your fault; you were just a handy target". That comforted me a bit.

I regained my composure and left for the cow pasture. Others stayed and drank from the dipper before returning to finish the ballgame. His rule changed that day to "consequence only". I think possibly the chatter among the stick ball players at the well wasn't to his liking. I don't know what the neighbors thought about the water bath, but I do know that everyone on the porch was quiet for some time after that.

Stick ball players drank and soon returned to enjoy the game. We <u>did not</u>, however, go for more water on that hot Sunday afternoon, July 1942. We drew our own conclusions independently. Stay out of Rasty's space if you want to avoid a water bath at the well.

Breaking the Huffman Academy Rules

During the 1920's to 1960's Barbour County, West Virginia had ninety elementary schools, most of which had one room, one teacher and a student population of twelve to forty five students. The Huffman Academy (my term for Huffman Elementary) was located in Huffman Bottom, about a mile plus from our farm. All the brothers and my sister, Betty, attended and graduated from The Huffman Academy. There were nine of us. At one time, during my first year, 1941-1942, there were five members of my family enrolled. In addition to the five of us, there were two dogs (Bud and Major) in attendance. Those dogs had already attended five years before I started first grade. They were there for another five or six years before they went on to dog heaven. Needless to say, they were highly educated dogs. While I'm on the canine population, I do not remember other dogs in residence at The Huffman Academy. I don't know why? Bud and Major were privileged I guess. They were allowed in the school, slept most of the day by the burn side stove and enjoyed recess and lunch breaks with us too. They were great watch dogs and alerted the teacher whenever anyone approached The Academy. They also passed gas occasionally; from innocent to a powerful olfactory challenge. Kids would hold their noses and snicker and point at one another, placing blame on an innocent girl or boy. Sometimes that was the high point of the day. The reaction for being blamed turned into pure theatre!

121

Huffman Academy Students -- 1939

During my seven years at The Huffman Academy I had five teachers and liked every one of them. In first grade I had a female teacher, Miss Nell. She became my first love outside the home. She would spend time with the four first graders, teaching us the alphabet and numbers, coloring, drawing, and later on reading, etc. At the end of the school day she would keep me a few minutes after others had left, give me a treat and kiss me farewell. I was special and I knew it. As an aside to this romance, Miss Nell cut me a break one day. She had added another rule to her list of "Thou Shalt Nots" due to older students using more swear words and foul language. The rule was, any use of foul language on school grounds and you'd get your mouth washed out with soap, period, with no questions asked. She explained this thoroughly in the fall of 1941. Any questions? No. On that very day, guess who violated her added "Thou Shalt Not" rule? Me.

After all, someone needed to test the new rule. After school was dismissed and I had received the treat and a kiss (aaah), I joined others in the school yard. I had just learned one of my first verses of a song from one of the older boys (Gerald) and after crawling through the barbed wire fence surrounding school grounds I sung it. "Old black Joe wheeled around and shit on his toe." Miss Nell heard it from her post on the school porch. She knew it and I knew it – I had violated her new rule. Needless to say, I was one guilty puppy and was in an anxious mode throughout the evening and next morning. I really didn't want my mouth washed out with soap and more importantly, I wondered if my violation had wrecked my romance with Miss Nell. I was upset, nervous, and anxious (I didn't know the anxious word then).

I was plain scared that next morning, but nothing was said, done, or even mentioned by Miss Nell or the other students. There must have been some kind of code among the students; don't tattle or it's best to let sleeping dogs lie. I liked that code. I also learned that prayer worked and that God was truly by my side, because I had prayed and talked with God all night. Please God, help me on this one and I won't do it again.

My second offense under Miss Nell occurred during spring term in 1942. I was winding up my first year of school at The Academy and had made great strides adjusting to The Academy and the learning process. I felt like I fit in and was one of The Academy's star first graders. I had been teased and had had my behavior shaped by Miss Nell and older kids. There were about twenty students (first through eighth grade) enrolled at The Huffman Academy. In fact, I and four older brothers

(Harold, Don, Lewis and Hayward) accounted for one fourth of the students enrolled there. Harold and Don were in eighth grade, Lewis in fifth, Hayward in third and I was in first grade. They had set the tone for my protection and academic prowess. I didn't disappoint them. I didn't need further protection from other kids; family security saw to that. It was comforting indeed.

I have already explained Miss Nell's "Thou Shalt Not" rules and will give you a "picture" of my second offense. I felt almost grown during the spring of 1942. After all, I was seven years old, had hiked the one plus miles to school through the cold and snow every day, had dug potatoes, shucked corn and contributed to all other farm labor during that year. At The Academy, along with other first graders, I began to pick up a few of the older boys' habits such as using curse words like damn and other "church" terms (wrong context), etc. I also learned to stand my ground with boys my age and older.

On the day of my second offense, we were playing softball at noon time. I got called out at first base. I actually hit the ball pretty hard and thought I had made first base safely before the throw arrived. I was called out by brother Harold who played first base. Brother Don, who was on second base, agreed with the call. A few damns and swear words escaped from my lips and were definitely audible. I knew immediately that Miss Nell heard it. I had broken her rule yet another time. I was in big TROUBLE!

Lunch time ended and Miss Nell called me aside to tell me that I had broken her foul language rule and she would whip me after school. I was indeed guilty and was prepared to spend the afternoon stewing over being punished. I had had my share of whippings at home and they just HURT! I had not, however, been whipped by a stranger and didn't know what to expect. I thought about pain, embarrassment, shame, and most importantly about wrecking my romance with Miss Nell. I would have to suffer the rest of the day to find out! There was about two and a half hours left in the day for me to stew over my mistake.

Our last recess was given and all students scrambled to the school yard for more games and fun. I wasn't really into that play period and sat on a tuft of grass by the fence feeling pretty low. I wasn't looking forward to a whipping after school and worse, one at home later that evening. I was also thinking about my busted romance with Miss Nell. At my lowest point there on that tuft of grass, brothers Harold and Don came to my rescue. They were eighth graders and grown in my world at that point. When and if they spoke to me, I would listen and act accordingly; otherwise, I would get pounded into the dirt.

Lesson learned! They said, "We want you to go home now." "We'll take care of your punishment later." I didn't ask any questions and started the lonely journey home. I did look back a time or two and felt like a scolded puppy. As I rounded the curve, I looked back and saw Miss Nell ringing the bell to signal students that recess was over. All became quiet as the last student and Miss Nell entered The Academy.

I felt safe at that moment, but what about tomorrow? As I had rounded the curve it occurred to me that I had a more immediate problem. I can't arrive home just yet; Mom would "<u>know</u>". I took my time on that particular journey home. I studied nature, looked for arrow heads and threw lots of rocks at specific targets (imaginary enemies). I managed to arrive home a tad earlier than the older brothers; any earlier would have blown my cover.

The older brothers didn't tattle so I was safe for the moment, but what about <u>tomorrow</u>? I stewed all night and was less than comfortable thinking about what tomorrow might hold for me. When <u>tomorrow</u> arrived, it began like every morning did; chores, breakfast, lunch pail in hand and off to The Academy. Four older brothers were in the lead cracking jokes and poking fun at what a kid had said a couple of days before. I was lagging behind trying to muster up some courage for facing Miss Nell. It also dawned on me at that moment that I had not only broken the language rule, but I had also left school without permission. I was in more trouble today than I was yesterday! What's a seven year old boy to do? I could hide in Grandma's barn for the day. Oh no, that would make matters worse. Intuitively I knew this and quickly dropped that solution. <u>What to do</u>? I thought it through and concluded that there was only one solution; be a "<u>boyman</u>" and take the punishment. The "boyman" thing perked me up so I stepped right up with my four older brothers and marched across the school yard into The Academy.

As I took my seat and waited, Miss Nell looked us over. She gave the eighth graders their assignment for the morning and then worked her way up to the front where I and the first graders were seated. She smiled at the four of us. I thought at <u>me</u> for sure! It eased my troubled mind a bit and I was able to answer her questions before others had a chance to. I was the star pupil during our fifteen minutes on the recitation bench in front of Miss Nell's desk that morning. Things were looking up for me at that moment, but what about….?

The entire day went smoothly for everyone at The Academy that day. Even the dogs were on their best behavior; no dog fights or growls at kids. The dogs just lay near the back door, sleeping and dreaming, I suppose, about the next recess or noon break. The day seemed tranquil and pleasant throughout the entire day; however, when the day ended and the students were dismissed, I was asked to wait. My heart stopped momentarily. THEN – I got a kiss, a big hug, and a treat. ROMANCE HAD RETURNED!!

After basking in the sweetness of that romance for a few days, I finally got the courage to ask Harold and Don how they "took care of it", for me. Their response was, "We talked with Miss Nell after we sent you home. We told her that we had sent you home and that we would take the whipping for you". Aren't older brothers wonderful! Apparently Miss Nell listened and took them seriously. She rescinded the whipping part, commended my brothers for their gallantry and praised them for looking out for their little brother. She also said, "I'm proud of you Ball boys and glad to be your teacher". They had made points with Miss Nell, had saved my little butt, and more importantly, salvaged the romance. Thanks, guys!

Miss Nell left me at the end of first grade in 1942. I lost a great teacher, romance, and a person who had a profound and lasting influence on my life. I loved Miss Nell and still do. She set the tone for me to enjoy learning from first grade at The Huffman Academy to finishing graduate school at Indiana University.

Other teachers at The Huffman Academy were good teachers as well. I will relate a few memorable events and experiences under their tutelage. As an aside, I must mention a book titled "Summerhill"; a book that was a must for graduate students at Indiana University from 1968 to 1971. Its thrust was on open classrooms, few restrictions, attending class if you wished, non-authoritarian, and so on. The catch was that in order to move up you had to pass the regions (exams). I can relate to that book in two ways – open with few restrictions and passing the state exam to move on to high school. I'll begin with relating the restrictions.

Doc, a teacher at The Academy in third and fourth grades, must have been a man of vision and certainly before his time and "Summerhill". For example, we took several nature hikes during the year; it kind of felt like the VonTrap family in The Sound of Music. The school family covered lots of meadows, Glade Run (marine life) and numerous wooded mountains. It was about a four hour trip on each outing. We would carry our lunch and drink from springs or clear creek pools.

Doc, like all other teachers, scheduled two fifteen minute recesses (stretch breaks) which we stretched into twenty minutes, plus. And, of course, he gave us a dinner break from twelve o'clock noon until twelve thirty. The older boys, ten years old and older, took advantage of the open classroom atmosphere and would often go fishing in Glade Run. We had a marvelous time with our improvised fishing gear. It wasn't anything like "Shakespeare" or even "Zebco" rods we had seen in Outdoor Life magazines. No way. Our fishing rods were made from small saplings, usually maple, each about five feet long. For line we used twine string and a hook made from a straight pin. We actually caught horny chubs and hooked a mud sucker or frog occasionally. Of course we lost track of time and were too far away from The Academy to hear the hand bell or referee whistle used to call us in. Early on we thought we'd be reprimanded, but we weren't and began to stretch that thirty minute dinner break into slightly less than two hours. We were operating under "Summerhill" policies and didn't know it. When we discussed "Summerhill" at Indiana University I couldn't understand the professor's excitement about such a remarkable school structure. The open policy at "Summerhill" was revered and viewed as visionary in paving the way for total reorganization of elementary schools. My professor was totally shocked that I had already lived the "Summerhill" experience during the 1940's at The Huffman Academy. I was called on a lot to relate The Academy's open door policy. That course was my favorite.

Another experience at The Academy, under another one of my favorite teachers named John, would occur during late fall of 1945 to 1946. John would bring his shotgun, a Remington pump, to school and leave it in his car. At dinner break he'd retrieve the gun and leave one or two older students in charge while he went hunting behind the school building. He would also have two older boys to accompany him on a squirrel or deer hunt up a small run in the woods. We loved it! We learned to be quiet, hunt with our teacher, retrieve game (sometimes a grouse), and most of all enjoy spending about an hour in a beautiful fall colored woods. In today's world, John would be arrested and put in jail for having a firearm on school property. He would most likely be sued for endangering children too. Oh, how things have changed. At that time we thought nothing of a gun in a car on school property. Everyone owned guns and hunted for wild game.

I could share many memorable experiences and incidents that took place while I was in school at The Huffman Academy as well as The Moatsville Academy, including Christmas plays, snowball fights, and cardboard sleds. A particular incident that comes to mind is when a kid named "Bud" peed his pants and made small paper boats to throw in the puddle on the classroom floor. Why, you might ask, did Bud do this? It was because our fifth grade teacher, Mr. Cornwell, refused his sixth request to visit the outhouse.

Another incident at The Moatsville Academy that I can vividly recall occurred in the spring of 1947. We were scheduled to play a softball game at Tacy which was about eight miles south of Moatsville. Transportation was a real problem so how were twenty-five school children going to get over there? Mr. Cornwell devised a pure and simple plan. He would take two loads of kids in his 1946 Chevy Pickup. He'd take the younger kids first while the older kids would start walking and be picked up later. We walked the first two miles and he didn't return for us, or so we thought. I, in my early leadership abilities, made the following suggestion; "Why don't we, about ten of us, just walk over the mountain between Route 92 and Route 38?" That one and a half mile over the mountain would get us closer to the pickup site. (We didn't even know where the pickup point was.) They followed my suggestion and we came out on Route 38 within two miles of Tacy School; it took us a good thirty minutes on that short cut. Very shortly after we had reached Route 38, Mr. Cornwell arrived from his third trip to Moatsville and back. Needless to say, he was not a happy camper. He let us have it! "I told you to stay on the road". God must have been smiling on me one more time, because not a single fellow student tattled on the decision maker.

We quickly piled in his pickup truck. I rode in front with one other kid. I was on guard and didn't want a possible interrogation in that truck to reveal my misguided leadership. I had learned from six older brothers on the Annon Farm how to protect my rear. We arrived to a warm welcome and felt like we were the pros entering Yankee Stadium. After all, we were the older kids and had played lots of softball. We won the game for Mr. Cornwell. He was proud and forgiving. He devised a new strategy for transporting the players and younger kids home. He brought the players home first, dismissed us and then went back for the younger kids. We all learned something important about communication that day; clear communication is needed in all situations and always be aware of rogue leaders, because you never know where, how, or when they may emerge.

Sixth grade at The Moatsville Academy was enjoyable. My interests expanded beyond baseball, basketball, swimming, hunting and a Barlow knife. They soon included girls and honing up my leadership skills.

As for girls, one cute black headed girl named Barbara, all of ten years old, had a crush on me. She let it be known and wrote Barbara loves W.B. on every large rock halfway up our road. She wrote it in white chalk. I tried to cover those inscriptions with dirt and mud. I wasn't quite ready for that romance and didn't want others to think that I had written that stuff nor did I want Dad to see the blatant inscription - BA LOVES WB. I don't think he ever noticed, because he never said anything.

Now back to seventh grade at The Huffman Academy. Cousin John and I were in the seventh grade together. We continued the noontime fishing trips up and down Glade Run and played lots of softball, tag, fox and geese. We went ice skating, sledding, and also enjoyed noon hunts with John S, our teacher. We continued to be inquisitive, inventive, daredevils, and just kids growing up in a remote protective environment in our corner of Barbour County. There are so many events and experiences from my time spent at The Huffman Academy that I could describe. What a place, what a time, what a family outside the home. I'll elaborate on a few, but I'll try to spare the reader's patience and prevent boredom from possibly setting in.

We were in timber and coal country which meant we had access to materials and activities that would be considered sinful and outlawed today. Slabs from the sawmill a quarter mile up the run, black powder fuses from the coal mines, and other various materials were coveted and used in our extracurricular activities. We carried slabs and scrap lumber from the saw mill and built forts. Each army would use "ammo" (snowballs) to attack the other fort. Of course there were open windows and large cracks where snow splattered the enemy. After snow season we planned out and made a small cannon. We'd seen cannons in history books when reading about The Revolutionary and Civil Wars. Black powder, matches, a block of wood, and a stem from a coffee pot were all we needed. We plugged one end of the coffee stem and soldered it; bore a firing hole near the plug and inserted the barrel through a block of wood. Now we were ready – we had the cannon and matches, but no powder.

Jonas Huffman lived nearby in Huffman Bottom. He had a small coal mine and black powder, so Bro Hayward, John, Jimmy, Raymond and I visited with Mr. & Mrs. Huffman at noon on a rainy Friday. It was wet and drizzling when we entered on the upper side of their porch. The floor was wet and slightly sloped to shed water that had splashed back from the water hitting the ground or from a wooden rain barrel. Rain barrels were common fixtures back then. They provided a ready water supply for washing, bathing, and watering livestock. We were wet, but invited in. They, of course, didn't know the purpose of this particular visit. We had often "just stopped by"; one never knew if any cookies had been baked! That was not our mission this time. I don't remember who the spokesman for the mission was, but whoever it was, they weren't very convincing and raised a heap of suspicion. In fact, Mr. Huffman said two things to us. "I don't think your teacher would send you here for black powder" and "you'd better get back to school before I whip all of you with my Black Snake Whip." "Mom (his wife), go fetch my whip." She rose from her chair and took one step, but we didn't wait around to see the infamous Black Snake Whip. We bolted out the door, hit the wet porch, slipping, sliding, and bumping into one another trying to leave and avoid "the whip". Four of us made it to the end of the porch; however, John wound up in the rain barrel.

He didn't drown and joined us later. John looked like a drowned rat, but was very happy he had not been introduced to that Black Snake Whip.

It took us until the middle of the following week to get over the Huffman visit. We didn't ask again, but were resourceful and located black powder from our other sources. I'm not at liberty to tell you where the powder came from; just from other resources such as shot gun shells, powder from one of the four homes represented, Mr. Huffman's coal mine, or we bought some from another kid. You take your pick. Anyway, we had powder and wanted to try the cannon.

We weren't sure if and how it would work. Would it explode in our faces or kill one of the smaller kids? We thought we'd better wait until the teacher and students had left for the day to do a field try. They soon left. I was the janitor at the time and usually swept the floor, dusted erasers, washed the chalk board and generally tidied up The Academy's premises, earning all of four dollars per month; therefore, I had a legitimate reason for being there after school let out. We figured John, Raymond, Jimmie, and brother Hayward qualified as helpers and it was okay for them to remain. After all, each of them had held the janitor position before and knew the drill.

In order to conceal our identity and the cannon, we decided to do the field trial inside The Academy. The first round would be fired with black powder only; second round would include a load of BB's. The next steps were to position the cannon and pick a target. We chose to place the cannon on a desk top and fire at the side wall with no windows. That was brilliant!

Don't fire at the windows. Believe me that was a tense moment even though we had weapon safety training and hunting experience. We knew what we were doing was dangerous. We'd seen a charge of black powder bring down a ton of coal from the face of a coal seam. There could be no mistake. We also knew about fire and other collateral damage, like leaving shots in the wall. We figured that wouldn't be noticed for a week or two. Little kids sat on that side.

We loaded and were ready. Next question was, "Who will fire the first round?" There were no volunteers until we removed some of the danger of that thing exploding in the volunteer cannonier's face. Two important strategies emerged from the experiment that took place that day. Number one was to place a stack of books between the cannon and the cannonier. A high stack of big books were installed. Number two was to use a long match to reach around the books from the back side. There were no long matches back then so we improvised and cut a long splinter from a red oak block; they split easily. Next, set it on fire with a regular match and light the cannon. I don't remember who the first cannonier was, but I certainly remember the second one. ME! The cannon was lit and went off with a loud noise while flames and smoke came out the correct end. We didn't know about giving high fives at that time, but there were definitely a lot of grins and giggles. We were now ready for the real test with a charge of powder and a load of BB's. Loaded and ready, next cannonier, please. "I'll do it" came out of my mouth and I did. At the time I was not aware of the increased risk; I was into the war thing and the south wall of The Academy was the enemy. I touched off the cannon and it fired. The flames and smoke seemed awesome! The shot hit the south wall and didn't like it; it came back on us, but there was nothing of any consequences, just a shower of shot. We had a huge laugh that time and felt we had succeeded. The three remaining soldiers took their turn at firing the cannon. We defeated the enemy that day and best of all left no BB's in the south wall of The Academy. We removed all evidence (BB's and cannon) from the premises and tidied up the place. I wonder if anyone smelled black powder the next morning. If they did, no questions were asked. With our mission accomplished, we retired the cannon and moved on to other adventures.

After mentioning cousin John in the above adventures, I am reminded of the fact that he and I started first grade together. There were four rising first graders in the fall of 1941. Two kids were held back after the third grade; one, due to a lingering illness and the other is unknown. Cousin John and I started school together and finished high school together. We were in every class together every day for twelve years. I don't recall the first heated argument or fight with John. We were "buds" back then and remain good friends today. Our lives have taken us down different paths and places, but when we do get together, which is rarely as we're three states away from each other, we slip back to our childhood days at The Huffman Academy.

I will relate one important adventure in the lives of Will and John. Like most kids growing up in the 1930's, 1940's and 1950's, John and I didn't have allowances, jobs as bag boys, newspaper routes, etc. Money was scarce. There was always Cloverine, Rosebud salve, and the Henry Field Seed Company. During the spring of 1948, John and I had an organizational meeting and did a "need" study for our three products. We had already sold Rosebud and Cloverine during the last two years. During our first year profits were marginal; the second year, profits were less than half from the year before. Our reasoning led us to determine that Rosebud and Cloverine just lasted too long and there was no reason to compete with their shelf life. I expect that some of that salve is still on the shelves of grandchildren of the folks we sold it to 60 to 65 years ago.

Seeds from Henry Fields were our product line for the spring of 1948. We also knew about the competition; other kids were selling seeds. We talked up the need for Cloverine and Rosebud around our sales competitors, but now we wanted to sell seeds. That was it! We ordered in the early spring of 1948 and sales were going well. We'd visit the surrounding farmers, display our seeds, discuss spring planting, (need to get them in early), sell a pack or two (15 cents per pack) and hustle on to the next farm. Our sales were mostly made at school during lunch-time. Remember the open/relaxed policies at The Huffman Academy? We visited farms within a one mile radius. What teacher today would even consider letting students venture that far? None. We did and loved every minute of it.

Back to sales and representing Henry Fields. John and I were making our last call one March day in 1948. It was an overcast, dreary and dark day; looked like snow clouds to us. We were about one mile up Tacy Road toward the Huffmans. We knocked and the door opened. We made our purpose known and were invited into their living room. There were the usual furnishings such as a pot belly stove, couch, oil lamps on a 2'x2' square stand, and a Sears and Montgomery Ward Sales Catalog lying about. Mr. Huffman invited us to sit and we did. Our sales pitch began and as we were taking seeds from the pouch, Mr. Huffman called the Misses (Roslyn) in to join the sales talk and see the seeds. She entered from the kitchen. By the way for two thirteen year olds, these people appeared fragile and old. They were in their mid seventies.

Mrs. Huffman was carrying the longest butcher knife that John and I had ever seen. She carried it close to her side; arm straight down, knife in hand with the tip of the blade ten inches from the floor. That threatened us a bit, but what scared the "bejesus" out of us was she kept it in her hand, laid it flat and sat down on it. We wanted to bolt, but didn't.

Believe me, it was difficult to finish our sales pitch, but we did. After all, we represented the Henry Field Seed Company and didn't want to let the home office down. The Huffmans bought some seeds. John and I liquidated all assets of our sales partnership after the last sale in 1948.

I've thought about the Misses' behavior quite a few times since. I think she was on to something. If all women today carried long butcher knives and sat on them, it would reduce assaults, robberies, domestic violence and improve the safety for multitudes. It would most likely slow down birth rates as well. Remember Lorina Bobbitt? You guessed it! I did not choose sales as a career.

Other Explosives

In addition to carbide and water in a bottle and a black powder cannon, there were railroad torpedoes and live ammo (12 gauge shotgun shells and twenty two cartridges). We were early adventurers into the world of I.E.D.s (improvised explosive devices). Our I.E.D.s were home grown and far less deadly than those used in the recent Asian wars - the concept similar only in improvised explosives. Our I.E.D.s were for the noise, not to injure anyone; however, we did put ourselves and others at risk occasionally. I'll discuss the railroad torpedo first.

The railroad torpedo was an explosive device used for signaling the engineer to slow the train down or stop due to problems on the track ahead. The torpedo was about two inches wide and two inches long; about a half inch thick with a lead strap through it. The lead strap attached it to the railroad rail. When the engine passed over the torpedo, it would explode; therefore, warning the engineer of problems ahead. Dad was a trackman and was responsible for setting torpedo warning devices when trouble warranted it. He would often have some left over and they were removed from his clothes on wash day. We'd watch for those, take them and plan to surprise someone within a day or two. A torpedo properly placed on a flat rock with a cap stone on top of it made a thunderous noise when a twenty pound rock was dropped from ten feet above. The explosion could be heard within one to two miles so we'd plan our surprises carefully. Rock ledges were plentiful and we knew where they were along most roads leading into Moatsville. Few cars traveled those roads; therefore, people walked the thoroughfares frequently. Rock ledges were perfect for dropping the "killer stone" and the understory growth made adequate cover for the surprise. I'll describe one such surprise.

Within a hundred yards south of our house was a perfect outcropping of rocks with ledges. The ledges were about fifty feet from the road; not much cover, but enough. Uncle Jim and Aunt Susie had a garden patch just across the road from our house. Their home was in a valley about a quarter mile below us. They would often visit their garden for planting, hoeing, picking, and so on; never just to inspect. We'd lay in waiting on the rock ledge, have everything in place, and have a forward observer out to see when they were on their way. We knew they were coming that day due to the local Bell Telephone conversations Mom and Aunt Susie had had earlier in the day. We'd be in position and wait. Aunt Susie and Uncle Jim would be walking along with tools in hand discussing their mission, paying no attention to anything on either side of the road. All was quiet on their trip until they passed the ledge. When the rock dropped on the torpedo below and exploded, everything changed. They were totally startled; hoes, buckets, seeds, and anything else they were carrying was dropped or flung on the road. We'd never witnessed either of them move so fast. They were usually in low gear walking, talking, and never in a hurry. We momentarily changed that behavior, but it didn't last long. When they recovered from the surprise, they picked up their equipment and supplies and continued on. The attack squad slipped out the back side through the woods and kept a low profile for the rest of the day. We returned to our farming duties on the other side of the mountain, discussed our success and laughed about scaring the bejesus out of Uncle Jim and Aunt Susie. Later that morning they stopped over at our house for water. They asked Mom if she'd heard the explosion. "Yes", she replied. "I think Bud E. is blasting rocks today."

We'd often pull that same trick on the Moatsville Community during early nightfall. We frequently felt it was too quiet down there, so let's go wake a few people up! We'd recruit a few friends along the way and plan where and when to wake Moatsville up. The planning seemed as much fun as the explosion itself. The explosion in that valley didn't rattle any windows; it did however, make lots of noise as it echoed up and down the Teter Creek and Glade Run valleys. We'd listen and watch for dogs to bark, lights to come on and people to come out on porches to investigate. After we saw all this and villagers cut off their lights, we'd slip away and quietly discuss the results of our mission. After all, we didn't want to disturb anyone with loud chatter or laughter.

Our other I.E.D.s were more dangerous. I'm surprised we didn't lose an eye, finger, or still picking buck shot out of our butts. We took greater risks and knew it. I later learned about divine intervention. In that situation, someone kept us from getting seriously injured. Those I.E.D.'s, twenty two and twelve gauge shotgun cartridges were always available. Dad and my older brothers had an arsenal of guns and ammo. We'd collect a few cartridges they didn't need (our justification) and experiment with the following activities. We liked noise;

141

we, being Rasty's "three little shits". I'll discuss the twenty two cartridges first. Twenty two's are small and were easier to confiscate from the ammo supply. They were not noticeable in a pocket. We'd take them a few yards from the house, find us a rock ledge, remove the bullet, take a hammer and begin striking the upright cartridge with the hammer. We would hammer it down as flat as possible and then the last hard blow would set it off. We liked the anticipation of the explosion and didn't think about the risk. The brass cartridge could and would occasionally send fragments somewhere else. We continued this risk for quite some time until Hayward broke protocol when he hit a cartridge and received a small piece of shrapnel between his thumb and index finger. That ended the hammer-explosion activity.

The twelve gauge explosive adventures involved more people and planning. We learned this one from our older brothers. It usually occurred on a rabbit hunt in winter time, with three or more other young boys. These hunts would last about six hours or more. About noon time we'd take a break, build a fire, and have a peanut butter sandwich; drinks were readily available from a spring or creek. Snow was on the ground in patches and it was cold. The fire was comforting to back up to in order to warm your rear side. We never did what Indians did. They made small fires and hunkered down close to the fire. Pioneers built a big fire and stood back. Maybe that saved us. After the fire had burned down, we'd had our sandwich, and were standing around the fire planning the afternoon hunt, one of the "little shits" would slip a loaded twelve gauge cartridge in the fire, then wait and watch the action. The twelve gauge cartridge would heat up, catch fire and explode. Shot and hot wood ashes would pretty much cover a six foot area around the fire. Life saving activities lasted a few seconds after the fire. Startled responses scattered the young hunters like a covey of quail. They stomped, slapped hot embers from their clothes, and slapped the back sides of others. After five minutes of safety measures and asking if everyone was okay, questions about what caused that and who did it arose. Of course no one fessed up. Could it have been a small rock? Rocks do explode if they get hot enough. They never knew. We pulled that trick a few more times, usually on a new hunter who would join us for the day. No one received an injury from the twelve gauge I.E.D. We were lucky, but I am not suggesting anyone try this.

School Picnics

In the 1930's and early 1940's, nearly every elementary school in Barbour County celebrated the last day of school with a picnic. The picnics during this time period at The Huffman Academy included the students' families, moms, dads, and other children who would eventually attend The Academy. It was a fun day. There was lots of food, deserts, and special dishes from the families. A variety of pop was furnished by the teacher. The bottle drinks were placed in Glade Run for cooling as no one had a cooler. Ice blocks had to be brought in for homemade ice cream. Electricity had not arrived in Huffman bottom just yet. There was a ball diamond there where the students challenged the teacher and parents to a softball game. Parent and student teams included any and all who wanted to play; women and men, boys and girls. It was a great day for the community and The Huffman Academy. Everyone enjoyed the social gathering, the softball game, and especially the food. There was always food left over. Some women exchanged the leftovers and their recipes while the men bragged about how good they "used to be" at softball. Everyone left with a full belly and parents were proud of their students.

As time passed, the picnics were not attended by parents or families. The teacher would plan an outing where he and the students could wade in a new creek, explore other native areas and fish in a trout stream.

The teacher furnished the hot dogs, drinks, beans, slaw and marshmallows. The students had a great time exploring new areas, creeks, rock ledges, tree climbing and riding the small trees over. At noontime we'd build a fire with wood gathered from the nearby woods. After the wood burned down, we'd burn the hot dogs and catch the marshmallows on fire. They were still edible and we thought they were great. After lunch we fished and explored even more. Everyone enjoyed the event and the last day of school. In May 1946, the teacher, one car (a 1946 four door Ford that looked like an egg), and sixteen students made the journey to a mountain stream above Meadowville; about a fifteen mile journey one way. How can you get sixteen kids in one car? Well, you can't. Six older boys rode on the running board outside the car hanging on to the inside of the doors and middle post; three on each side. Brother Hayward and I rode on the running board with four other boys. There were ten other kids inside; older ones on the seat with smaller students on their laps. Seat belts had not arrived yet. All safety rules in the County were broken that May day in the spring of 1946. Our teacher, John S., was one brave teacher and trusted that no one would fall or jump. We called him John and yet had great respect and admiration for him. In today's world he would have been sued for negligence by every parent for putting their child at risk, lost his teaching license and jailed by Social Services.

I enjoyed the picnic and thought the ride over and back was great. Not a single parent complained or approached John about the safety of their child. He kept his contract and returned to The Huffman Academy for my last two years there. John was a great teacher and provided us with basic educational and life skills.

I have great memories of him and our time together at The Huffman Academy. Thanks John.

Sleds and Grapevines

I sometimes think we tried to kill ourselves or harbored a premature death wish. Most boys and girls in the Allegheny Mountains owned a homemade bobsled and knew where every grapevine was within walking distance of their homes. Sledding was the favorite winter sport while swinging on grapevines was the sport for all seasons. Very few boys and girls owned a store bought steel runner sled so we usually made our own. Some sleds were short and some were long enough to carry more than two riders. I'll start this story with the grapevine swinging first.

Grapevines were plentiful; you just chose and cut. In order for a grapevine to hold a swinger, it needed to be an inch or better in diameter and big enough to grip and hang on to. We graded the vines as good or perfect. A "good" vine was strong and could easily hold one or two swingers; a vine you could swing out twenty feet, but wouldn't get high off the ground and one that was fairly close to the mother tree that held it. While we played and swung on lots of good vines, they presented a major problem. When you backed up with the vine in hand, ran forward and became airborne, the trip out was delightful. It felt good to be airborne and free as a bird; however, the trip back to the landing site wasn't as pleasant. Adjustments had to be made during midflight back or you'd slam back into the trunk of a mighty oak or beech tree. That would hurt! It only took one or two flat nosed meetings with the unmovable tree to learn how to make mid flight adjustments and miss the tree. We made adjustments in midflight and saved the noses.

The "perfect" vine was usually located over a deep ravine, rock ledge, or steep mountain side; one that would carry the swinger fifteen to thirty feet above the ravine, mountain side, or rock ledge. A "perfect" vine would also hold at least two swingers and travel thirty to forty feet one way. When we found the "perfect" vine we used it often. A vine one to two inches in diameter with branches high in a mother tree was preferred. We'd cut and test the grape vine for safety purposes; first one swinger, then two, then three. Well, you get the picture I'm sure.

I will relate four vine swinging experiences that I can clearly remember, including the visual pictures in "living color" in my cranial file. Two of these events cause me to break out in a sweat when I think about the unforeseen and potential danger involved. I'll start with the earliest and least dangerous.

Grapevines don't last much more than a year. They must be tested often for safety, especially for the little folks before they can swing. One such test was underway by brothers, Harold and Lewis during fall term at The Huffman Academy in 1941. That swing had been cut the year before and had given swingers many rides and much joy every day school was in session the year before. The swing was in the woods on the "Cellie Sprocket Farm" and as luck would have it, along the path to school; very convenient and unusual.

Swings were usually inaccessible and more remote. In any event, we (five brothers) were on our way home one fall day when we arrived at the swing site. I was in first grade and had limited experience on grapevine swings. The vine was a year old and needed testing before I could ride. The Pre-OSHA Safety Test was shortly underway. Harold and Lewis were the safety testers for the day; Harold in the eighth grade and Lewis in the fifth, grabbed the vine and backed up. They did the take off run and were quickly airborne. The flight seemed long and smooth until it hit the end point of the pendulum flight where swingers would switch direction and return. The vine decided it was finished with all trips and broke. The expression on two vine safety inspectors' faces was one of surprise and "Oh my God, we're falling!" Fall they did with arms and legs doing all kinds of contortions in an effort to land without breaking something. Luckily they didn't. They had fallen about ten feet in rather soft soil. Soft soil is rare in the Allegheny Mountains. They were lucky, and I was pleased that two future OSHA Safety Inspectors had inspected the vine that day before I tried it.

A second grapevine snap shot of a "perfect" vine involved brother Hayward. There were two "perfect" vines located up a ravine behind The Huffman Academy; one we could use in a Tarzan enactment. We could swing across the ravine and drop off on the other side, about a four foot drop, with both feet on the other side of the ravine; we could then drink guava juice with Jane. Obviously we had seen a "Tarzan" movie. That swing was a great one. Imagine letting your son or daughter swing across a twenty plus foot deep ravine, with no helmet, safety harness, or gloves to grip the vine. We did it without protection and never lost anyone in the ravine. We could also swing back if someone would send the vine back over. Great memories of that vine remain. How many boys have memories of swinging over to Jane's place in the jungle and drinking guava juice with her?

The other vine near The Academy was closer in and on an extremely steep mountain side. When anyone swung on that vine, they hung on for dear life. At the "turn back" part of the swing, the swinger was a good thirty-five feet off the ground; a big boy's only swing. No girls or younger kids allowed, period. We knew danger when we saw it.

Rasty's "three little shits" were on their way to The Academy one spring morning in 1945. We decided just one swing and then on to school. Hayward, being older, stronger, more athletic, and having shared more guava juice with Jane, decided he'd go first. We all dropped our lunch bags and were making ready for our rides. After all, we had also drunk guava juice with Jane, but just not as much as Hayward. Cecil and I conceded and the ride was underway. Hayward couldn't back up much and make a run because the mountain was too steep. In addition, he had to commit to a flight plan in order to miss trees in the flight path. He did all the necessary planning, gripped the vine, and was airborne. The swing and swinger were in harmony; a sturdy vine, a swinger with a huge grin and all was well with God and nature, at least until the end of the out trip. At that very moment and for reasons unexplainable, Hayward either lost his grip or was so enthralled with his flight and wanted to be launched further into outer space, he let go. He fell that thirty-five feet and landed on the steep mountain side butt first.

He slid a foot or two downward and was stopped by a stump between his legs. You talk about luck, miracles, and divine intervention; Hayward experienced some divine intervention that day. The only injustices were a busted lip when it connected with his knee and testicles rearranged by the stump he straddled to stop the skid. After we assessed the injuries and judged him to be mobile, we were thankful that he survived. Cecil and I decided we did not wish to swing that day. Why run the risk of a busted lip or worse, singing higher notes in "Mr. J's" music class that day? We made our way to The Academy that morning with no further discussion of the fall or with any thoughts of swinging on that vine on our way home.

A third picture of grapevine swinging occurred during spring of 1949. Leaves were setting on and warmer weather had arrived. Brother David and I were on one of our exploratory journeys on the "Glade Run" side of our farm. He had just turned seven; I was fourteen and grown. It's not clear to me what the exploration was about that particular day, but most likely it was a fishing trip in "Glade Run" or a yellow root foray. In any event, we did whatever the exploration called for and were making our way home up a steep mountain side. The timber had been cut two years before. A steep mountain side and slash cut timber allows all kinds of weeds, trees, and briars to regenerate; all that makes for a hard trek up the mountain. We would walk, rest, and figure out the next best way around treetops, briars, etc. Walk, rest, and figure, walk, rest, and figure. We were nearing the top when we spotted a "good" grapevine. Why not swing? After all, we'd had a hard climb and needed a rest anyway. Boys always carried a <u>Barlow</u> knife back then. I cut the vine with the

151

Barlow and tested the swing. It swung out over tree tops that had been left from the timbering operation two years before – a good ride twelve to fifteen feet off the ground and twenty to thirty feet out. I made a second test; back up, take a few fast steps forward and off for the ride. I enjoyed both rides. Brother David was waiting and getting excited about his turn. I held the swing for him and gave him the safety talk. He listened and said he could do it. I thought I was a good instructor on grapevine safety. After all, I had seen two near death experiences and had drank guava juice with Jane on the other side of a ravine before swinging back to reality on the other side. What better training for safety and enjoyment on grapevine swings would you want?

David was ready! He gripped the grapevine with a seven year olds' grip and took off. He was having the ride of his life. At the far side of the ride he let go. I couldn't see his face, but I expect the expression on it was a realization that he had bailed out and left his parachute at home. Needless to say he made a crash landing in a large tree top. I had never witnessed sky diving without a chute before, nor had I heard so many limbs break in succession. After breaking through seven hundred limbs, David hit the ground with a muffled thud.

My mind was in panic mode. I could see him with broken bones, legs, arms, a broken neck or worse, skewered on a broken limb. I was responsible for his safety and I was panicky! I didn't go around anything getting to him, I went through it – briars, limbs and any other object between us. I was yelling, "David, are you hurt?" "Are you hurt, David?" I had forgotten the David and Goliath story and the luck that David had in slaying Goliath. Davids are special you know. I was concerned about "brother" David. By the time I reached him (about three seconds), he was standing and brushing himself off. He was a bit dazed no doubt, but mostly okay. I was so relieved that he wasn't hurt or on a skewer that I didn't even say, "I told you not to let go". We left the crash site and continued our journey up the mountain. We arrived home from the "Glade Run Foray" and had increased our knowledge and experience in grapevine safety. That may have been my last swing. I don't know about David's continued interest.

What about Sleds?

As I mentioned earlier, sledding was the winter sport of choice. We were not familiar with snow skies at that time; that came later on with television when we learned about Switzerland and other winter sports. We did, however, invent a form of snowboarding; a form not yet discovered with competition in the Olympics. Maybe they will catch up later? I'll explain "our snowboard" later. Very few Steel runner sleds existed in our greater community. Greater meaning at least three farms between us in any direction. I vaguely remember Edith and Jimmy owning steel runners. Steel runners were much smaller than the sleds we made and didn't carry as many riders. Our sleds were made of seasoned oak and had three main pieces; a front steering section attached to the rear section with a six inch wide board. The board was permanently attached to the rear section and attached to the front section by a bolt. The bolt allowed the front section to swivel and guide the sled. Long wooden sleds would give up to four sledders the ride of their life. They sat on the sled and held onto each other for "dear life". Your life was in the pilot's hands. Some pilots were more daring with their crew than others. The daring ones purposely wanted to ditch the ship and they often did.

Now for the sledding areas. It wasn't difficult to find a long or short slope that was steep or less dangerous. The bigger problem was finding a slope without too many rocks. The other issues for bobsleds and steel runners involved the amount of snow and the temperature; too much snow, the sled wouldn't go; too warm, it wouldn't go then either. A good cold five to six inch snow in freezing weather was best. We'd get quite a few of the "ideal" snows throughout the winter months in Barbour County.

At home we had our regular runs which were mostly short. Remember, we didn't have lifts or assisting devices to help pull the sled back to the top, nor was there any lodge for warming or nursing a broken leg. You rode down and you pulled the sled back to the top. If you felt like pulling the sled back, sometimes we'd get daring and sled down the country road which could be half a mile. Shorter runs seemed safer and more fun.

At The Academy we had the best runs ever. The Academy sat at the base of a steep hill. The school yard was one acre fenced with barbed wire. That wire wasn't there to keep us in, but to keep the cattle out. "Nobles Hill", as we called it, came right down to the porch side of the school building. The distance between the porch and fence was about twenty feet.

What I'm attempting to describe was a dangerous obstacle course for sledders. Let's continue. The run would start from the top, middle, or lower portions of the run; it depended on your risk tolerance or strength of the death wish. Remember the fence twenty feet from the porch, the barbed wire fence perpendicular to the run? That meant you would make the run, go under the fence and make a quick right turn to avoid hitting the porch. God, I don't know how we survived those runs! As to the fence, we had about five feet from posts on either side and five strands of barbed wire. That spot had been used by former death wishing sledders and had been worn down about a foot lower than areas between other fence posts and barbed wire. The distance between the ground and the lower strand of wire was two feet. That was too dangerous for two sledders. One lying on the sled could make it and this was in our safety manual. If two were to ride, one on top of the other, lying on the sled, the safety manual required us to unhook the lower strand of wire. That gave us an additional foot of clearance and no one would get their head severed. We had a quarter mile steep run straight down to the school. Sledding down the slope, under the fence, making a right turn and coasting to a stop without killing some kid playing in the school yard was considered a good run. We'd assess the run and go again. We did this year after year at The Academy without getting the first head severed or without killing some innocent kid in the school yard. God was looking out for those with death wishes as well as the innocent kids in the yard.

Looking back, I'm certain we picked the most dangerous run to rev up our adrenaline, rise to the challenge, take a dare, or more than likely try to impress anyone who watched the death riders. I don't know if Hells Angels were any more daring than we were. I also question, why "there" when there were so many good safe slopes in "Nobles Field". All we had to do was move the run a couple thousand feet to the right and it would have been longer, safer, and easier to pull the sled back up the hill. What were we thinking? I guess we were following the earlier death wishers. I'm glad I'm alive! Those runs were dangerous! No bull.

Our "Snowboarding Invention", called a "snowboggan", was probably a hybridized version of a short snow board and a toboggan. The snow board we used was a twelve inch wide, ten foot long rough sawn board we confiscated from the local "pecker wood" saw mill. We selected carefully. It was nice and flat with a good turn up on one end; just enough turn up to slide over the snow. We slatted the board with twelve inch long by two inch wide slats positioned about two feet apart to keep board riders from sliding forward. Our snow board would hold five riders comfortably, but ten was more fun; the more the merrier. Ten riders seldom hung on from top to bottom. In addition, the more snow the better the ride; sledding for eight inches or less and snowboarding for anything above eight inches. It was a lot more fun in snow over a foot deep or even more.

Your fate was in the hands of the person up front, the pilot. There were no steering controls; you would lean left for left or lean right for right. We got better when we learned to point right or left so riders could lean with the pilot. Little kids loved it and would sandwich in between the older kids. Riders on the snow board were much safer. The snow was deeper and served as a cushion when we had a spill. Those rides were never straight down the sled run. We knew that even if we could hit the open space under the wire fence we'd slam up under the School porch and that would be sudden death for all riders. Even worse, there could be six to eight angelic student riders shredded and tangled in the wire fence. Can you imagine six to eight kids hitting a barbed wire fence at forty miles per hour? It was risky enough for two kids on a sled to do the straight run. At least on a sled there were only two risking their lives. On our "snowboggan" there would be six to eight funerals. Besides, if six or eight kids lost their lives, the school board would close The Huffman Academy.

Sledding and snowboarding at The Academy was great sport. It built trust in the pilot and bonded The Academy family; however, I do shudder today when I think of the risk and danger involved. The Huffman Academy was not the only school to enjoy grapevine swinging and sledding. I expect every school and student in the county has their stories which would match ours. They may not, however, have tried as hard to kill themselves.

Paul Bunyan and Babe

Most young boys were fascinated with the frontier life and adventures of Paul Bunyan and Babe. It may have been required reading for fourth graders at The Academy's library. The library at The Academy consisted of one unabridged dictionary and about thirty books encased in an oak book shelf with a glass covered front. How those glass doors survived is beyond my comprehension. I was ten years old, in fourth grade and had read the book. As a matter of fact, Paul and I had become good friends and explorers. When I cut fire wood, bean poles for the garden, or small logs for a fort at The Academy, Paul Bunyan and Babe were there to help. I and other boys would cut four inch diameter trees and have "Babe" drag them back to The Academy yard to construct a small log cabin. I was Paul and other fourth graders were "Babe". I had three "Babes" to drag the logs out. We built an eight by eight foot cabin and a make shift fence around the cabin to keep the Indians and bears out.

As you might have surmised by now, I was the leader of the fourth grade pack. They may have been the smarter ones, because I did all the chopping, selecting and placing the logs in constructing the fort. It's easier just to carry stuff and drop it at the laydown site.

As I indicated in other stories, my chore at home was keeping the wood box full of kindling and fire wood for the cook stove and the "Burnside Heating Stove". That required lots of chopping and splitting. It always felt better if the box was full and my chore was above par; just a personal self-assessment here.

On one occasion, I was chopping and splitting a long hickory pole that was about six feet long and three inches in diameter. I had cut it and dragged it from the woods nearby. It had been carefully selected to make a bow. I had made several bows and arrows by that time, but this one was going to be bigger, stronger and better. On that particular day, I really felt strong like Paul, chopping and splitting that wood. Sister Betty was still at home and about eighteen years old. She and Mom were in the house cleaning and cooking for the "men folks". I, on the other hand, was Paul Bunyan, splitting the Hickory pole top to bottom. Things were going pretty well for Paul B. until, for some unknown reason, "he" decided to start the splitting in the middle of the pole; not the ordinary from top to bottom split. Starting the split in the middle just seemed manlier. Hickory is hard to split regardless of where you start. I started in the middle because Paul B. would start there and with his strength he could stick both hands in the split, ripping it apart and ending up with one half in each hand. It was underway. I'd chop and pry, chop and pry, until I had about a three foot split midway in the pole (Paul B would have called it a log). A couple more chops and I decided with my abundant muscle and strength I could stick my hands in where the axe was stuck and rip the pole apart. I did the usual mind over matter to gain extra strength and it actually worked for a brief moment. I pulled hard and opened the split wide enough for the axe to drop out. The pole retaliated and closed back up with my fingers locked inside. It hurt!

I didn't want to yell and admit defeat, but it really hurt! The pain didn't ease off and I had to do something soon or I'd lose my fingers. That Hickory pole was gaining strength and I was losing it. I still didn't yell or scream. I picked up the pole in front of me and went to the house. Can you imagine what that looked like? Here standing at the screen door was an eleven year old Paul Bunyan with his fingers stuck in a six foot pole. I'm sure I wasn't smiling when I asked Betty to help get me out of this thing. Can you imagine Paul B. asking an eighteen year old girl for help? My dignity was shot! It hurt and I didn't want to go through the next two to three years waiting until I gained more strength to rip that pole apart so I asked for Betty's help. She didn't laugh then; maybe later. Thanks Betty. She had me lay the pole on the chopping block so she could put the axe back in the split and pry. Thanks Betty for not whacking the split with the axe! She pried and I was released. Free at last! Free at last!

That twenty minute episode seemed like a two hour ordeal to me. After the feeling in my fingers returned, I cut the Hickory pole into fire wood length and enjoyed watching every piece of it being fed into the cook stove. "Take that, Mister finger biter!" I continued my Paul Bunyan adventures after that, but was wiser and a little more selective. Lesson learned!

Often on a Paul Bunyan hunting excursion I'd have a rifle and two farmer type matches. Usually after a rain, I'd tramp through the fields and woods looking for squirrels or rabbits. If it's too wet to work, go explore; what freedom for a young boy! After an hour or two, I'd challenge myself (Paul B.) to build a fire and have one match left. Building a fire in wet woods was definitely a challenge and the self-imposed restrictions (one match) were more so, but a good frontier woodsman could do it. I'd look for dry "punky wood" under a tree or in a hollow log, and of course, the Barlow knife was great for making shavings to start the fire. I must say it took some planning and gathering dry wood stuff before the match was lit. I'd carefully pick a rock ledge for the fire. There were three reasons for this; one, it would provide a dry base; two, it was less dangerous in setting the woods on fire, and three, it provided a place for Paul B. to set down and admire the fire. After thirty minutes of prep work, I'd light the shavings and nurse the fire to life, from shavings, punk wood, to small sticks, etc. Paul and Babe felt successful and enjoyed the flame and heat.

I'm only one of the many hunters who built fires to get warm while on a hunt during the winter months in the Alleghenies. Today, young hunters probably don't need to build a fire to warm them. Why? They ride four wheelers through the woods, have insulated everything, socks that are battery powered to warm their feet and warming packets to place in their gloves. And besides, they wouldn't know about a Barlow knife, punky wood, and one farmer's match. In addition, who would trust an eleven year old boy with a knife, matches, or a rifle in today's world?

Peckerwood Sawmills

"Peckerwood Sawmills" were plentiful in the Alleghenies during the 1920's to 1960's. There were six of them within a two mile radius of our home in Barbour County. Peckerwood Sawmills were small privately owned and operated. The owner was usually the sawyer and employed one to four helpers. Two helpers cut timber by hand with a cross cut saw, one helper snaked the logs to the mill with horses, and the fourth helper would "off bear" as well as remove slabs and lumber from the carriage. Timber was plentiful up to the 1960's, but became scarcer in later years. Most farms had some timber and would sell it to the independent sawmill owners. Both the seller and buyer added income for their families as well as a day's pay for the sawmill helpers. Helpers were often family members, relatives, or friends; they were a tight knit group. Sawmilling was not a "pie" job; it was hard work and dangerous for man and beast. Tree fallers ran the risk of a tree kicking back, dropping a limb or more hazardous, falling on someone. Logs are heavy and hard to move. If you attempt to roll a log on a truck or skid for the saw it could always roll back on you. OSHA would have gone "stark crazy" with Peckerwood Sawmill safety, or I should say the lack of it. When folks talk about "sawmill dollars" they are talking about how strenuous it was to earn a dollar.

Sawmills near our house that I recall were owned by Annons, Appersons, B. Bolyard, H. Bolyard, Leaches and Polings. There were more in the Laurel Creek area and elsewhere. Peckerwood Sawmills were plentiful up to the 1960's. Today, I don't notice very many as I drive through the West Virginia mountains. Small operations have given way to larger more modern mills where logs are graded, sorted and stacked for further processing. That's progress and progress often eliminates jobs for the locals as machines do more and more of the work. Go figure! Are we better off with sawmill progress? I'm not sure.

As a young boy in the 1930's and 1940's I was fascinated with the sawmill operations in our area. One mill closer to us was the Poling Mill. I would sneak off and go down to the mill and watch the logs being processed, turned from a dirty black log to peach colored boards. I studied the total operation and could have run that mill myself at eight years old. One thing that fascinated me most was the two belts; a large wide leather belt with a twisted loop that ran the saw and a metal conveyor belt that removed saw dust from under the large circular saw blade. The metal conveyor belt was small, about four inches wide with scrape blades that were about two inches tall. It was driven by a sprocket and pulled dust out from under the saw blade forty to fifty feet. They would change the direction occasionally and spread the saw dust. Saw dust piles were marvelous places to play in, roll down, wrestle in and dig holes. Afterwards it was hard to get the saw dust out of your clothes. It felt like sandpaper inside the clothes and made the walk home more abrasive. Most of the saw dust was gone by the time I got home and aside from being sanded by it the experience was well worth having your skin removed.

One of the benefits of having mills in the area was that if boards and construction lumber were needed, it was close at hand and the price was right. Farmers would negotiate with the saw mill operator and goods would be delivered for a new building or repairs within a few days.

Rasty's "three little shits" asked for and were given permission to take trim boards from the mill. Trim boards were thin boards that were left behind when the sawyer squared up the log for sawing into lumber. Trim boards were usually thin on one end and thicker on the other. We used these boards to build play houses. We built three small shacks and played in our village which included a store, post office, and the Mayor's house. The shacks were roughly constructed. Each had a small door for access and privacy and was large enough to hold three small kids inside. We had a great time building and playing in our village until one of the older brothers (Don) unloaded a twelve gauge shot gun on our village. Luckily, no one was home. Rasty's "three little shits" didn't like that at all; however, Don was older and had seniority. We let it ride and soon turned our "homes" over to Mom for biddy houses.

Years later, brother Don also shot down a biplane that I had made and placed on the barn roof. It was a weather vane and rotated to show wind direction. We called biplanes double wingers. At that time, Cecil and I were building stick model airplanes and some would actually fly. Rubber band powered flights were short, but very enjoyable. It was exciting to actually build a plane and have it come alive in flight. We imagined we were in the plane and flying it. We had quite a few good flights, smooth and long, but nevertheless, crashes were common. We as pilots would climb out of the crashed plane, assess the damage and make the necessary repairs. Brother Don didn't shoot us out of the sky, although he wanted to, and we made sure he wasn't around when we flew our planes.

I mentioned the double winger weather vane plane earlier. It was a beauty! It was painted with a silhouetted pilot flying it on top of the barn. I could hear the propeller running at night. In addition to the biplanes, I and other kids made toys, sling shots, carvings, etc., and used them in our activities. Every boy worth his salt owned a Barlow pocket knife and could carve. After brother Don shot my plane off the barn, I missed hearing it and seeing it turn with the wind. It was not repairable, nor did I carve another airplane. I did not want to provide any more targets for brother Don; shooting up our village and shooting me out of the sky in my biplane was enough for me.

I wonder if kids today would be interested in building and owning a village or making their own toys. What an adventure and learning experience for three young enterprising kids, Rasty's "three little shits".

I have also wondered about other "little and/or big shits" in our area and how they came by their "schitt" names. The following schitt names were given to some of these folks: chicken schitt, O'schitt, dip schitt, pisa schitt, dumb schitt, loda schitt, deep schitt, giva schitt, fulla schitt, awe schitt, old schitt, holy schitt, no schitt Sherlock, knee deep schitt, jack schitt, and that's about all I know about the schitts. If you study the schitt relatives and neighbors a bit, one would begin to make the connections. Will Poling labeled "Rasty's three little shits" sometime during the early 1940's and it stuck during our early years. It bothered brother Hayward considerably, but Cecil and I coped and let it pass. We knew it was a term of endearment! We didn't tell brother Hayward until years later that it was a term of endearment. After all, he liked the cod liver oil and let Mom know when she forgot to give it to us at bedtime so we just let him stew over the "three little shits" label.

Several of the Schitt folks mentioned above worked on the sawmill crews and earned good reputations for their endurance and work ethics. They were well respected; however, once they were dubbed Jack schitt, it stuck for life. They, as the three of us, learned to laugh and live with our nicknames. As to the cod liver oil, Cecil nor I continued taking it after leaving home. I'm not sure if Hayward did or still does, but he liked the stuff! Yuck!

Church, God, and Rasty's Three Little Shits

Church and God were important institutions in everyone's life in the Alleghenies. Old and young alike recognized and respected the church and the Lord. Some of the churches in our end of Barbour County were The Evangical United Brethren at Fairview, the Methodist Church in Moatsville, the Nondenominational Ritter Church at Moatsville, Old Road Church in Moatsville, Saint John's Methodist, Mt. Morris, Locust Grove and the Shiloh Church of the Brethren at Kasson. Shiloh, at one time, had satellite churches at Colebank, Moatsville (Nicklow), Hickory Grove and Union Chapel. There were several other churches in the area, but I don't recall their name or denomination.

My church, our church, and church families were close knit and the social connection for mountain people. Churches and the one room schools were the gathering places for gossip, news, budding romance, philosophical and religious discussions. There were other spirited activities and young kids would attend church with the parents starting at an early age. From birth to leaving home in search of work or being drafted into the military, young and old alike took religion and faith seriously. We used lots of church words in conversation, "God will get you for that", or in other contexts when we were upset, riled or just plain mad. Church words just flowed freely during those episodes. We'd ask for forgiveness afterwards and of course someone would remind us of the Ten Commandments, "Thou shalt nots"!

Here are two examples of how God and religion was woven into the fabric of young people in the Alleghenies during the 1920's to 1960's and beyond. Anyone living in North Central West Virginia on June 23, 1944 would most likely remember one of the most devastating tornados to hit the state. It touched down in Shinnston and several other communities in West Virginia before it reached the Virginia state line. The storm hit our area late that evening around 8:00PM. The storm moved in fast. The clouds were dark with open spaces in them where orange to red color streaks showed beneath the clouds. Lightning and thunder abound and was enough to keep the youngins on the porch. We usually enjoyed running through the rain on hot summer days as it was refreshing, but that night was very different. Cousin John and I were only nine years old at the time, but even at that age we sensed danger. What we and other family members were looking at was eight to ten miles south of our mountain top farm. Early on we did get wet, then hail started to fall; small hail at first, then larger hail later on. The first hail was about three quarters of an inch in size. It was strange. It wasn't round, but instead it was shaped like someone had chopped it off a stick. From the end it looked like it had annual rings, much like a tree would have.

I shall never forget Cousin John's comment; "I can just see God up there chopping up that ice". For a nine year old boy, wet and scared, that was a perceptive comment and good description of the hail. Later on the hail was much larger and round, almost baseball size. Dad measured one hail stone at eight inches in circumference. That was dangerous and kept us on the porch. At that time we were not forewarned of a major storm in our area, because it was before television and radio warnings. I'd never heard of a tornado, but this one got everyone's attention. The next day we heard about it. A relative or neighbor took us and others in a pickup truck to Meadowville to see where the tornado had touched down. Houses, barns, automobiles and livestock were scattered and turned every which way. The most digging feeling for me was the sight of cattle taken from their barns and tossed on a hillside. Some had timbers in them and it looked like cows stuck on a huge pin cushion. My thought was what caused this horrible destruction?

One hundred people lost their lives in the Shinnston tornado. No lives were lost in the area we had looked at that day; however, we learned a few days later that others had lost their lives in the surrounding area. Needless to say, that storm got everyone's attention and churches had great attendance afterwards.

A second event that describes the influence religion had on us during the spring and summer of 1944 in-cludes several characters. The main ones involved in this event were brothers Hayward, Cecil and of course me. Others will be introduced as the story unfolds. The scene in this event includes our area, the house, Moatsville, and The Fairview EUB Church.

Cecil, Hayward and I were nine, eleven and thirteen years old; better known as "Rasty's three little shits". These "three little shits", my older brothers, and my sis-ter Betty would attend Fairview with Mom for Sunday school and revivals. Sunday school for the "three little shits" was taught by Nett M. She'd start a lesson, "Now when Jonah was swallowed by the whale"....... Within five minutes we'd learn about <u>her</u> operation, how the doc didn't numb anything anywhere, jerked her around and said, "Quit whining, this isn't supposed to hurt." Doc cut the thing open and it took two hundred stitches to close the wound. He charged her four dollars and told her to take two aspirin and return in two weeks to have the stitches removed. We always thought the next week's lesson would include Jonah being up-chucked on the beach and Nett M. revealing her life threatening scar. She never did and needless to say, we were disappointed.

Monte G. was the minister at Fairview Church. He gave one sermon a month and performed funerals and weddings as they occurred. He was a veteran of WWII and a prisoner of the war. He was for real. A born again Christian. God got him through the prison ex-perience and I believed then and still do that neither you nor I can fathom what that was like. He gave us a "peep hole version" of what life as a prisoner of war was like for him. His message was so strong and from the heart that he had some of the hard shelled folks (those that didn't express their belief openly) attending revivals and church. When you could get Rasty, Poppy P., Fl A., E.E., J.A., and H. H. to attend church service and to utter a word, God was surely there. Bless Mon-te G.

The Fairview Church was about one mile south of us; Moatsville about one mile north. Moatsville was a small village with three churches and two small family owned stores. These two locations are paramount to this story. A description of other characters in this story will soon unfold as well.

170

<u>Cheet was the self-appointed Mayor of Moatsville</u>. He was ever more vigilant of all happenings large and small. He knew every person that lived in the area, including young children. He just did because that was his job. He was an old man in 1946, or so it seemed to me at eleven years old. He did get older before giving up his high office. Cheet and his wife, Rosie, lived in a log house. I liked that house. It had low ceilings and a water pump in the kitchen. We would go there to get water for The Moatsville Academy. My tenure at The Moatsville Academy was for one year from 1946 to 1947, but more about that later on.

Cheet would meet his Mayoral obligation daily, walking the roads, greeting folks old and young, as well as collecting and passing on all the important information and gossip to anyone willing to listen. His house and yard were strategically located for his work. It was next to Galls General Store where there was always a hub of activity going on. His yard was level which is unusual for West Virginia. It had been built up about eight feet on the lower sides and contained by a heavy cut stone wall. The stones were laid on the road side as well, tapered from eight feet on the lower side to nothing on the upper left side. There were concrete steps midway up the road side; four steps up to a landing, turn, and four steps up to the walkway leading to the house. The yard was nicely landscaped, but I don't know who did it. I doubt it was Cheet as he was too busy with his Mayoral duties.

In the high corner of the yard was a maple tree which provided shade for the Mayor's chair and observation post. He could see seven roads coming into the village. Anyone on those roads was spotted long before they reached the Post Office or either of the two stores.

He was on duty daily. Need I say more about the Mayor? I'll speak of his observation and advice a little later.

<u>Emil S. was the local news reporter</u> and indeed the owner of a small printing press. He wrote and printed local happenings and upcoming events monthly in a two page 8 ½ x 11 Crier. He distributed it by placing a few Criers in each local establishment. He was also pleased to give them to anyone passing by his print shop. Emil was a rather quiet man which rendered some folks unsure of his motives or thoughts. On his behalf, I as a young teenager, found him to be gentle, thoughtful and lonely. He would invite me and several other teenage boys to his shack to play a card game called Rook; usually a couple of evenings per week. He also included a small story about the <u>Moatsville Coon Holers Band</u> in his "Town Crier". He would send the information to the <u>Barbour Democrat</u>, a weekly newspaper out of Philippi. The band members, Willard, Ron Ritter, and I were eager to see our names on anything. And of course, that publicity made us famous! I don't, however, remember getting too many gigs from the publicity. Emil would also invite us to practice at his shack and that made the news print as well. I think he also liked seeing his name in print. He and we would take any recognition we could get. We were typical teenage boys; when you got recognition and praise, you liked it, but weren't sure what to do with it.

Part of those mixed feelings were probably due to folks telling us and others, "don't let it go to your head" or don't get the "swell head" over your accomplishments. We were humbled by this.

The Three Little Shits, Hayward, Cecil and Will --
"member to be" little brother, David.

One of the residents in Moatsville was a master at "cutting you off at the knees", so to speak. This particular resident was a large woman that was very vocal and often offered her opinion and critique without invitation. We tried to avoid her as much as possible, but she was a master at just appearing at locations where one (we and others) could be cornered with no quick escape route available. It was hard for her to assess the impact she inflicted on others, know when to let it pass, or just shut up. I hope these character sketches give you some understanding of those great Americans from the

1940's and 1950's.

Now on with "Church, God and Rasty's Three Little Shits". We were mostly well behaved, thoughtful, and knew our station in the scheme of things. However, we occasionally broke bad and created recreational and self-directed activities that might not please the church crowd. I'll cite a few for you.

I've already elaborated on spitting on the Ritter boys' bare feet which of course wasn't nice. I don't know why they didn't retaliate or lay in waiting with sticks and stones the next time we walked by their house, but they didn't and we continued to spit.

Moatsville had two bridges; one was a cement WPA project over Glade Run and the other was a larger metal bridge over Teter Creek. It had weight limit signs on both ends indicating nothing over 20 tons. For young boys with sling shots and plenty of small throwing stones available, the signs made for a prime target and we would shoot and throw rocks at these signs at every opportunity. If it was dark, we used heavier artillery, such as baseball size rocks. We paid little attention to the small print on the bottom of the signs – government property-federal offense. We were also unaware that the Mayor was observing and taking notes during these escapades.

Another incident involved a young Moatsville native who was a bully of sorts. He was at our place one early spring to pick up free cabbage plants and while he was there he began picking on me. I was eleven at the time and he was thirteen. He wasn't aware that when you do that, the whole pack of brothers will come after you. He nailed me with one or two punches and threw me

174

to the ground. That was enough; he had crossed the line. Brother Hayward came to my rescue; he was also thirteen. He grabbed the bully (the Mayor's grandson), threw him across the porch banister and I whipped him with my leather World War II Ace Pilot's flying helmet. The helmet had goggles and straps on each side that closed under the chin. When it was snapped together under my chin, I couldn't lose my headgear in a straight down bombing dive. I whipped that bully pretty hard with the Ace Pilot leather helmet and we sent him home with battle scars, no doubt.

The next evening, Dad was returning home from work when the Mayor stopped him to discuss the problems his "three little shits" were creating in and around Moatsville. Dad and other Railroaders always caught their ride to work at Moatsville at five thirty each morning and arrived back there about five thirty each evening. Dad would still have to walk one mile up our mountain to get home. The Mayor spoke to Dad concerning the spitting incident, our destroying government property with slingshots, and more importantly how we had ganged up on his grandson and had bruised his behind. The Mayor waited for a response from the tired railroader. Dad's response was, "I'll take care of that when I get home. I'll whip them." The Mayor wasn't into corporal punishment so he offered an alternative. "It might be more effective if you had the Reverend Monte speak to them. You might want to think it over." Dad had the mile hike home to mull over his suggestion; he did and mellowed some before getting home. There's something to be said for a long walk up a mountain.

Once Dad arrived home, he discussed these issues with Mom and they later arranged a meeting with Reverend Monte for Thursday evening after supper. Rasty's "three little shits" weren't privy to the arranged meeting so there was no time to prepare our defense. Supper on Thursday was the usual spread for the Reverend; two meats, three vegetables, biscuits, cow butter, jelly, and a desert. The Reverend said the blessing; a long one that involved repentance for sins and blessings for a bountiful harvest. We were not aware what was on his agenda for the evening, but we certainly liked the bountiful harvest part of his prayer. It was on the table in front of us. We were hungry and anxiously dived in. The Reverend liked the harvest too. He took his time and ate heartily. We finished long before he did and waited patiently. During that time period, kids didn't leave the table until the adults completed their meal and a second cup of coffee. Sometimes that took "<u>forever</u>"! Finally, everyone had finished and we were ready to leave the table and go play catch or some other important game. Mom quickly stopped us and told us the Reverend wanted to talk with us. Whoa! What brought this on we wondered. We'd already been to the Reverend's Revival and been saved. Had we back slid?

In any event, we were stuck. The Reverend excused Mom and Dad and told us to wait while he had a few words with them on the porch. He probably let them know he'd be more effective going it alone. During that brief word with Mom and Dad, brother Cecil had disappeared. He was a skinny kid and made like a shadow. He vanished! The Reverend either didn't miss his presence or decided the two older "shits" needed his counsel more anyway.

The Reverend sat down across from Hayward and me. We were pretty glued to the bench behind the table. The Reverend began by telling us that we were God's children and He expected us to be respectful of other people and property. He then began to relate the sins of spitting on people, destroying property, and fighting. He elaborated on these events and had obviously been well informed. We had no defense and fessed up. By then the Reverend was into his preaching mode with sweat on his brow, a handkerchief in hand and getting louder. He had the "bejesus" scared out of us. All of a sudden, he slammed the table with his fist! The sugar bowl, salt and pepper shakers, and dishes remaining on the table did a jumping dance and then came to a rest. The Reverend then in a loud stern tone said, "Where's God?" – pause – "Where's God?" Needless to say, he had our attention.

The Reverend then stood up, sweating profusely, and hit the table again, repeating with authority, "Where's God?", "Where's God?" He then turned and left. Hayward and I were briefly stunned. We were alone in the kitchen, free to go and we did. We thought we'd better find the other "little shit" and knew where he was. He was hiding in the open clothes rack in the back bedroom and was concealed pretty well. The only thing exposed was Cecil's bare feet below the long dresses, coats, etc. He parted the clothes, stuck his head through and asked, "What's going on?" Hayward and I in unison said, "<u>God's lost</u> and <u>they</u> think we had something to do with it!"

That session with the Reverend was quite effective. The "three little shits" didn't spit on the Ritter boys' feet anymore and didn't have to bruise the Mayor's grandson again. We knew he had learned a lesson and wouldn't mess with the Ball Boys again. As to the signs and other available targets, we just got more selective.

Years later I related this story at a family reunion as it seemed like a good time to fess up before God and family. After I finished telling the story, my brother Cecil informed me that he didn't remember some of the events. Of course he didn't. I reminded him that he had hid in the closet, called him slick, and asked if he remembered hiding. "Yes", he said. I also told him that Hayward and I carried the load for him that evening because he was our brother. What greater love than love for a younger brother is there? I also said you were an important member of Rasty's "three little shits", so we protected your membership and Mom, Dad and the Reverend never learned that you missed the entire "God's Lost Sermon". The Reverend was so into the sermon that he didn't even miss the lamb that disappeared. I've since wondered about a shepherd who wouldn't miss one lamb out of a flock of three. Neither Hayward nor I ever tattled so Cecil was safe. I've also wondered if Cecil needed the "God's Lost Sermon" anyway. He has served God well through his church and layman activities without even knowing that we were instrumental in "God Being Lost" that evening in July of 1945. Kids have so much influence, don't they?

<u>Bell Tower Project at Fairview</u>

Mom, Will and grandson, Tyler -- 1990.

The Fairview Church was our church and we attended there on a regular basis for Sunday school, preaching, revivals, funerals and weddings. Henry Annon, my Grandfather, was one of many in the community who helped build and finish the church in 1909. The steeple held a large bell which rang for church services on Sunday morning and tolled for emergencies and deaths. A large rope came down through a hole in the ceiling and was looped over a hook; easy access for ringing and for boys to ring and swing on as they pulled and rang the bell. Most boys tried it and sometimes would sneak in the church, if in the vicinity, and give the rope a tug. Of course the neighbors within ear shot, about a mile or more, wondered what one ding from the bell meant. A few people checked on the one ding occasionally, but I think most already knew. I don't remember for sure the number of tolls for a death, but I'm thinking it was three.

Ward and Burl loved that rope and would beat everyone to church for Sunday school. They rang and swung, rang and swung; no limit on rings for Sunday school and preaching services. They rang and swung.

The Fairview Church was built in 1909. It had been through some extreme hot summers and cold, cold winters. There was no central air or heat to stabilize the wooden structure. The only climate control device in the church was a potbellied Burnside Stove located dead center of the main isle. To my knowledge, no one had ever checked on the bell tower supports for the bell or the condition of a one inch diameter rope that rang it.

Ward and Burl arrived early one Sunday morning and were in the process of ringing the bell to invite any and all for Sunday services. About the second ring and swing thing, the rope had had enough and broke. It broke at the bell and about thirty feet of one inch rope and a swinger hit the floor. There were no major physical injuries, just pride; however, thirty five years of dust and fiber floating down was something to see. What to do? In that predicament a typical reaction for boys was "get out of Dodge". If I'm not standing here in tangled rope, no one will know. Ward and Burl bolted out the door, cleared the church yard, crossed the road through a second gate and kept running for home. They were almost out of sight of the church when they met their parents, Jerry and Net. Marty, their uncle, was walking with Jerry and Net. "What's wrong?" Out of breath and scared they said, "The bell rope fell out of the ceiling. We heard noises in the bell tower. It made a swish, swish, sound after the rope fell. We want to go home!"

Like all astute parents, Net and Jerry didn't buy it. They turned the twins around and marched them back to the Fairview Church, assessed the situation, and had the boys coil the rope and sweep the floor. Sunday school went on as usual. Of course there was talk about ghosts in the bell tower and who was going to fix the rope. Typically in our community, if you broke something, you fixed it. There was no money to hire someone to fix it for you. In this situation one or two people couldn't reattach the rope. In addition, the rope was thirty five years old and had been exposed to the elements as well. The usual church protocol took place and a committee was formed. The repair committee met for decisions and planning; who, what, where, when and funds for a rope were settled. On the appointed day, Jerry and five other men, plus the twins, arrived and began the repairs. They set ladders on the outside as there was no access from the inside. The steeple had louvers on all four sides. The louvers had no screen to keep out bees, bats, birds, and insects. Can you imagine thirty five years of accumulation?

The repair day had arrived and repairs were underway. First question was, who will be the first hero to go up the ladder to remove the access louver and replace the rope? Some discussion followed. "I have a bum knee." "I'm allergic to stings." Isn't everybody? "I'm afraid of heights, etc." Two brave men stepped forward;

Bud E. and Uncle Sammy. Bud was in his forties and Sammy was in his sixties. Both were war veterans, climbers, carpenters, and general do it yourselfers. Matter of fact, everyone was a do it yourself person in those days. They tied pouches full of tools around their waists and the climb began. There were two ladders; one on the ground, the other on the roof, tied down and secure. Each ladder was manned by the ground crew to hold it in place while the heroes climbed and worked.

Bud and Sammy were able to stand on the roof ridge near the bell tower. It was a two man job. One ladder wouldn't hold two workers. With hammers and pry bars they began prying the closest louver off. There weren't any cordless drills and screw drivers back then. I'm not even sure screws had even been invented yet. Everything was nailed shut. Bud and Sammy hit the pry bar with a hammer to seat it and began to pry the louver out and off. They woke up every hornet, wasp, bat, and other critters living inside. Bees started swarming around the intruders' heads. Sammy and Bud were swatting at bees and trying to keep their balance on a steep tin roof. They received a variety of stings while swatting and holding on for dear life. Sammy began a diatribe of biblical terms, mostly out of context. Usually Sammy was a laid back, easy going gentle soul, but at this moment he wasn't. He was in battle with the bees and was angry! He was inventing new curse words and was hot under the collar, so to speak; cussing up a storm while fighting those blasted bees. Bud, in the middle of the fray, said, "Uncle Sammy, have you forgotten where we are?" "You'd better pipe down or the Lord will snatch you bald headed." "What in the hell do you mean?" replied Sammy, as he yanked his hat off and said, "The S-O-A-B has already done that!"

Sure enough there wasn't any hair within three miles of Sammy's head. He was a total <u>chrome dome</u> – Yuel Brenner type; nothing there to snatch. They quickly left the duty station to rethink and reorganize the bell-rope situation.

Sammy and Bud, the heroes, were not going to be defeated. They copied a marine strategy and advanced to the rear to plan their next approach. The plan was to wait until dark when all bees and other critters would be bedded down for the night. Then they would spray the little devils. There were no pressurized spray cans in those days, but there were small pump type hand held sprayers with a tank to hold the insecticide and a pressure tube with a pump handle. You held the pressure tube with one hand and pumped with the other. If you had a good sprayer, it would deliver the insecticide about three feet; good for flies, but not so much for bees. This worked well when standing on a flat surface, but was more difficult off a ladder or steep roof. Armed with the sprayers Sammy and Bud were on the roof after dark and ready for the second bee battle. Thank the Lord it was a moonlit night, otherwise, who would climb the ladders and hold the flash lights? The heroes sure couldn't. They had both hands on a sprayer and spray they did, starting with the most difficult side and working back to the ladder. They did this without too much fanfare from the bees. Surprise is a great battle plan. It worked and Sammy didn't have to invent additional cuss words.

Heroes, helpers and the twins returned the next morning and began removing the access louver and attached the rope to the bell. They encountered lots of dead, sick and hold out armor-plated bees. You know the kind that just won't die! They gave them an extra dose of insecticide and went on with the mission. They attached the rope and dropped it through the hole in the ceiling and reset the louver. The mission was accomplished. They recovered ladders, tools, and then sat down to relive the episode; what, when and where they had made good or bad choices and if it's ever done again the twins would do it. After all, they were apprentices in training during the last two days.

The last item of the rope project was to knot the end of the rope for gripping and ringing the bell and to place a sign where the hanger held the rope. The sign simply said, <u>PLEASE DON'T SWING ON THE ROPE</u>. Ward and Burl took the pledge.

The Banana Caper

In the spring of 1947 brother Cecil and I were twelve and eleven years old; trustworthy, dependable and almost grown for that era. We were dispatched to Galls Store in Moatsville to purchase two 100 pound bags of cracked corn. Cracked corn was mostly used for chicken feed, but occasionally other livestock received a handful or so as a special treat and it helped catch the horses for a cowboy ride. Can you imagine riding a sixteen hundred pound work horse bareback in a full gallop? More about that later. The mission for this day was to pick up the feed, put it on the horse in front of you and get it home. There was no "be careful", "don't hurry", "you'll get a treat when you get home" stuff, just go and fetch!

Pretty simple, huh. Yes, but when a ninety or one hundred pound boy has to load a one hundred pound sack (they were cloth and flexible) of feed on a horse that stands over five feet high, "Houston, we have a problem". Two of "Rasty's three little shits" were quite resourceful. We were always resourceful and sometimes to a fault. We always knew how to manage. The feed was kept in a small storage building on the south side (upper side) of Galls Store. The saving grace was that it had a loading dock near the road so we could get the horses close and load the sacks on them. Guinevere unlocked the building and showed us the cracked corn. We rolled two bags on the floor, carried them down 3 or 4 steps, and dropped them on the loading dock. Our next chore was to get a one hundred pound bag of feed on the horse's back and keep it there. We knew if we missed the mark and dropped the bag that most likely it would burst. We really didn't want that to happen. After all, we were trusted, responsible and almost grown men. We led both horses, Molly and Polly, one behind the other over by the platform. They were on their best behavior and stood where we stopped them.

The first loading episode was easy; two boys lifting and sliding the bag on the first horse. Once on the horse and with minor adjustments, the bag adjusted its shape to fit the horse's back. If you have equal weight on each side of the horse, the bag stays in place; at least right and left. Forward and back creates a problem if you are traveling upgrade. We would be doing that shortly. We managed to load the second bag pretty smoothly, thanks to a sleeping horse dreaming of greener pastures after the one mile climb back to the Annon Farm – theirs and ours.

Cecil and I climbed aboard our horses behind the feed. We were well aware of our responsibility to keep the bag on the horse. Side to side wasn't much of a problem; however, front to back, mostly back on steep climbs, would be the greatest problem. Remember, we weigh ninety and one hundred pounds and the cargo in front of us weighed one hundred pounds. The first half mile was no sweat, but as we began the steeper grade rounding the John A. curve, the trip became rocky and steeper each step of the way. The banana caper began to unfold. I pulled a banana from my pocket and took a bite. Cecil was curious about that banana and asked if that was on the purchase order. We were into the steep part of the John A. curve at that point where the horses were working harder to climb the grade. I was in the process of "fessing up". "No, it wasn't on the work order, I took it". Took was a euphemism for stole. At that very moment (God apparently didn't like the words "took it") the horse took an extra long step forward and I, along with the feed, slid off the horse's rear and landed on top of the rocky road. Not only did the rocks beneath me hurt, but a one hundred pound bag of feed covering me up didn't help much either. While God's punishment for my actions that day was painful, He was also a loving God. The feed sack held and we didn't have to scoop it back in the bag. By the way, I never did finish that banana. I really didn't like bananas for a long time after that.

We managed to reload the bag, pull the horse to the high road bank and with new found strength (fear) we placed it on the horse's back. We arrived at the top of our mountain without a welcoming party or fanfare. We unloaded the feed in the storage building and turned our faithful horses out to green pastures where their dreams became a reality.

I have reflected a bit about the "Banana Caper" and have drawn two conclusions! Number one, that taking things that don't belong to you will work on your conscience long after the fact and that the "thalt shall nots" are helpful social standards that keep societies glued together. Without standards, we would have total social decay. Number two, that my demonstrative behavior, learn by observation and doing, impacted brother Cecil greatly that day and ever since. How so you might ask? Well, as Dad would say, "I'll tell you".

To my knowledge, Cecil never took anything without asking first; no hard core theft, never cheating others out of their valuables, and lives by honesty as the best policy. Cecil has a deep abiding faith and uses Christian behavior in all things. He provides music and song for his church, church leadership, and lay ministry to all. What a testimony for a brother I dearly love.

I do believe that God and I during the "Banana Caper" in the spring of 1947 planted the seed and shaped Cecil's behavior in order for him to do God's work. I think God and I work well together.

The Moatsville Coon Holers

Music was a part of life in the Alleghenies. Most families listened to the W, W, Va. Jamboree out of Wheeling, the Grand Ole Opry out of Nashville, and the Renfro Valley Barn Dance out of Renfro Valley, Kentucky, on Saturday night. Old and young alike would gather around a battery powered radio and listen. They would make a few comments about the performers and who was liked best. Out of that music sprang some wannabe musicians. A few families owned musical instruments and learned to play by ear by listening and practicing, then copying the picking strokes until they could play the melody and sing the song.

Brother Carl entertained full time for a few years in the Baltimore, Shenandoah Valley and D.C. areas. He would also play gigs with friends locally when he was home for the weekend or on vacation. His love for music rubbed off on me. I purchased a Silvertone Guitar for twenty-four dollars from Sears in 1950 and struggled to learn a few chords. If you knew three accompanying chords and what goes together to form a key, you were well on your way to stardom. Carl would show and coach me until I learned the Mel Bay method which consisted of 3 chords. He invited me to play a few local shows at churches and family reunions. I was so nervous I'd shake head to toe and struggle through it. He'd go back to Baltimore and always encouraged me to keep practicing.

I kept at it and also found two other budding musicians, Willard and Ron, in Moatsville. Willard played the mandolin and Ron played the guitar. We practiced about three times a week and felt comfortable with a few of the 1950 country songs. Then we took our show on the road. We played in one of the local stores on Friday nights and at homes when invited. Our biggest gig was at the senior play at Kasson in 1953. We received applause for our performance and an Emil S. write up in the weekly Barbour Democrat newspaper. It was exciting to see our band's name, <u>The Moatsville Coon Holers</u>" in print. Up to that time, we had not chosen a name for our band so Emil named it for us – "The Moatsville Coon Holers".

The "Coon Holers" did play a couple of times at Poling's Bar on Route 92. They would provide a hat or jar for donations and invite us back. Sometimes we'd just show up and play. One time when we played at Poling's Bar, we were packing up to leave and someone took the tip jar. That didn't set well with us or Mr. Poling, but we enjoyed our performance more than the customers anyway. The last time we played there they threw us out. I'm not sure if it was because we were underage (all of us were under 18) or because we sang "Everyone's Got F__t Stains in Their BVD's". That song seemed okay for the men folk, but may have been too risqué for the women folk. Anyway, we were asked to leave. We've had a few laughs over that since. After that event, the "Coon Holers" split; two of us graduated and moved on seeking employment. It was a great time and place for three budding wannabe musicians. I expect there were several budding musicians and singers in most hollers, valleys, mountain tops and small villages throughout the Alleghenies. We did compete once in a musical talent show for the Kasson F.F.A. Chapter at Elkins and came in third place. Some of those bands were pretty good and more polished. I still have that third place white ribbon somewhere.

I have often thought about how resourceful mountain folks really are. They didn't complain or get bored. They were inventive and learned to entertain themselves through music, telling stories, naming people and staging a prank now and then. This statement about resourcefulness must be somewhat true beyond the borders of West Virginia. A neighbor from eastern North Carolina told me, after a gig, that I had surprised her. She also said how much she enjoyed people from West Virginia, because they were always full of surprises. I thanked Elizabeth for the compliment.

As you have no doubt gathered from these stories thus far, I have worked hard to provide a good model for Mountaineers to follow.

The Moatsville Candy Heist of 1949

There were a few Moatsvillains in the Moatsville area from its inception to its present day. I have heard about theft, robbery (mostly hams, grain, cattle, sheep, timber, etc.) and a couple of murders – one of them being my grandfather. Most Moatsville residents were very forthright, hardworking, and just good people.

I don't know of all hanky-panky events or people; however, I do know or have heard about the sneakier, sly capers, time, place, parties involved, victim and perpetrator – little stuff like that. I and most folks in our small community were well aware of any Moatsvillain's shady record. Folks just knew the under belly participants and their methods. After all, moonlit nights cast long shadows and people remember.

I will share a Moatsvillain episode. After sixty plus years I feel safe due to the statute of limitations and because I have confessed before God several times since. Repentance is such a great tool for erasing guilt. In addition, I feel okay because Galls' Store has long since been closed and removed from where the incident took place. Also, the vendor has passed and I'm too old to be jailed at this point.

I was with the accomplices that moonlit night in February 1949. I will not use names, only made up initials so I can protect their identity and keep characters straight for the writer and reader.

It was customary for young boys to gather at Moatsville in the evening after chores were completed. Winter, summer, spring or fall, we would show up and hang around, mostly on a cement bridge spanning Glade Run. We'd sit and visit from about seven in the evening until sometime after nine. We weren't into politics, national disasters, or even events at the County Seat of Philippi, West Virginia. Television and other media like Newsweek and The New York Times had not reached us by the spring of 1949. We did, however, have a battery powered radio and would listen to local news and weather reports. A major thing for most families was ear to radio on Saturday night music programs – Grand Ole Opry, W.C.K.Y., Wheeling Jamboree, etc. Our discussions were about important stuff such as why we couldn't catch the "big fish" in Glade Run or Teter Creek, you know, the "big one" that got away. We also talked about our baseball and basketball skills and where we'd swim on Sunday afternoon; the Moore Hole in Teter Creek or the Blue Hole in the Tygarts Valley River? These were important discussions by young teenagers from a different time and place.

The "Candy Heist" took place in February of 1949. That was one of the "cold snow everywhere" months. There were three of us and no one was sitting on the bridge. It was way too cold! We were throwing ice and snow over the bridge and watching it float away; fun stuff like that. About seven o'clock it was already dark. The sun had set at five and the moon was shining brightly above making it easy to find your way in the night.

The following was not my plan; I would not have considered it; however, mob psychology was and still is a real phenomenon. I must admit I was easily drawn into the "heist" that cold night in February. We spotted a small delivery truck with bread and snacks coming down the old road; not the paved road on the other side of Teter Creek. The bridge spanning Teter Creek at that time had washed out and was not safe. The truck coming down the old unused road was probably on the roughest dirt and rock road in Barbour County. The driver was working hard to dodge mud holes and big oil pan puncturing rocks; otherwise, the driver would be finding a "tow horse" or replacing the motor within a few miles. That road was rough indeed!

The old road on the south side of Teter Creek was the first road to Moatsville in horse and buggy days back in the 1700-1800's. It actually was passable, but rough. It also sported a fording spot about one mile upstream. It was the only thoroughfare into Moatsville from the north side of Teter Creek while the bridge spanning the creek was out and being repaired.

I only mention the road to acknowledge the driver's efforts in delivering his wares. He had to be careful, drive slowly and dodge the obstacles to safely deliver bread, candy, crackers, cookies, and nickel bags of Planters Peanuts to Gall's store. Upon seeing the delivery truck arrive at Galls Store, three underbelly agents devised an experimental plan; in plain English, theft. "B" laid out the following plan as he seemed better organized. "W" and I listened. We would hustle up the road, find a shadowed spot where the road was rough and then wait. When the driver arrived, we'd emerge from the shadows and run up behind the truck.

"B" would open the doors at the rear of the truck and climb in. "W" and I would trot along behind and handle the goods (candy) when "B" handed it out. Staying out of the driver's mirrors was easy. He would be too busy trying to keep the truck between the ditches and dodging rocks and mud holes.

We followed the plan and laid in waiting under cover surrounded by bushes and Hemlock trees. The truck arrived, we quickly were in place behind it, "B" opened the doors, and the Heist was underway. We had three minutes of the rough stretch of road. After that, neither "W" nor I would be able to stay with the truck. Slick "B" was in the truck and had no time to be selective. He grabbed three cartons of candy bars and handed them out to the accomplices. He then jumped off, caught up with the truck, latched the doors and stopped while we watched the truck disappear. Now that was thoughtful of "B" to lock the truck's doors to prevent further loss of goods when the driver forded Teter Creek about a half mile upstream.

I don't know which brand of candy "W" and "B" received that night, but I wound up with my favorite candy bars, a 24 count box of Zagnut. They are my favorite still today; however for some reason they are not quite the same.

The Zagnuts went home with me that evening (23 of them). We each had one candy bar from our boxes in honor of a successful mission. Before I got home, I had plenty of time to think through what had just happened. Believe me, that one mile hike up the mountain was sobering and it took longer to get home that moonlit night. I had stolen something, had joined the ranks of

Moatsvillains, and had to figure out what to do with the stash. I couldn't share it, because that would certainly raise suspicion and some questions about finances. I had no money, they knew it. I devised a plan. My plan – I would hide it under my bed and have one Zagnut every third day. I would have to eat the candy bar away from the house and others who might detect my Zagnut breath. I ate lots of snow to cover that. It must have worked because Hayward, Cecil, nor David ever asked where I found the candy.

I guess that lets me know why none of them went into law enforcement. Please don't misunderstand. I am not suggesting theft of any sort and by all means, do not try it. God and I made peace about the Heist. It served as a valuable lesson for this fourteen year old in 1949.

I will close this exposé on The Moatsville Candy Heist of 1949 by sharing a song I wrote about it in "The Moatsville Candy Heist of 1949". Enjoy. See Appendix.

The Blue Hole

Streams and rivers were places of adventure, recreation, and excitement in the mountains of Barbour
County. Our recreational area covered about a two
mile radius and included Glade Run, Laurel Creek,
Teter Creek and Tygart Valley River. We spent days
exploring, fishing, ice skating and swimming in these
water ways. The area that was explored the least was
Laurel Creek. There were a couple of reasons for this.
It was further away and Mom didn't like us out there.
She didn't give any reason other than she didn't want
us to go. Laurel Creek was a beautiful creek and me-
andered through the valley for about ten miles. I don't
think it was any more dangerous, but Mom knew it was
in or closer to boot leg liquor operations and she was
adamant about her dislike of "spirits" and didn't want us
to start drinking the hard stuff. Apple cider was okay,
but moonshine was not! We didn't disappoint her and
stayed clear of Laurel Creek most of the time.

Our favorite swimming hole was the "Blue Hole" in
Tygart Valley River. We usually swam there on Sunday
afternoons. The brothers and I would invite friends and
have a great time swimming, jumping, and diving off
rock ledges on the west side of the river. On the east
side of the river was a nice sandbar; a small beach
where we could rest, roast wieners and marshmallows,
and lay on the warm sand. During the 1940's and early

1950's it remained undiscovered by the city folks from Philippi. It was our private beach and only we enjoyed it. Of course the locals knew about it and would visit, but during that time there were never more than a dozen people swimming there.

The Blue Hole beat any Olympic size pool ten-fold. It was over two hundred feet across and about a thousand feet long. When we left the sandbar and swam out a short distance, we had thirty feet of clear water under us. The water was clear and very cold. It took a good swimmer to dive down and bring something up from the bottom. On good sunshiny days, the entire body of water was blue and clear enough to see the bottom. It would have been a great place for canoeing. None of us owned a canoe or small boat; we just swam there.

We practiced our swimming skills and would race to the other sides and "crow" about winning the swim race. While on the other side, we would practice diving off the rocks and ledges, taking our pick as to the height, anywhere from 8' to 40'. The forty foot dive was done by very few divers. Toad Reed and I would take turns and show off from the forty foot perch. Most of the other boys would hold their noses and jump off. The ledge on that side of the river ran the entire length of the "Blue Hole". The ledge averaged 10' to 15' in height. The forty foot height was created by a huge boulder that had rolled onto the ledge from some place up the mountain. My guess is it rolled there before the river carved the channel. Otherwise, the boulder would have rolled into the river. What an enchanting playground for young people to use. Our group did not vandalize or trash the place. We swam, jumped in, dived in and picnicked there often. Occasionally, parents would come and spend the afternoon with us. We really showed off for that audience. I expect other youngsters in the Alleghenies had their favorite swimming holes and playgrounds and have wonderful memories of such special places.

During our time at the "Blue Hole" no one was hurt or drowned. Since leaving the area in the mid-fifties, the "Blue Hole" was discovered, vandalized, several injuries have taken place, as well as shootings and drownings (about one per year). Now rafting and canoeing have taken over that section of the Tygart Valley River. If that's improvement, I'll not visit and I'll live with my memories from the 1940's and 1950's. What a place and time for young folks to grow up. We didn't know how blessed we were to have the "Blue Hole" for our recreational pleasures. Oh, what memories.

Will and Hayward -- 1952.

Romance and First Dates

Our area in Barbour County, West Virginia, was sparsely populated, rocky and rough. It was the northern part of the county and the last part of the county to be settled. Indians remained there longer than other nearby counties. Our area was truly "Wild and Wonderful West Virginia".

The young folks met at socials, church, school, family reunions, weddings and funerals. The serious stuff between boys and girls began mostly at the onset of high school. There were fewer boys if you were a girl and fewer girls if you were a boy to choose from; fewer in that we were very picky and chose carefully who we wanted to spend time with. I expect our selection process was universal, but perhaps a bit more limited. In looking back and making an observation, one difference may have been that once the choice was made, and sometimes it was early on at fourteen and fifteen years old, it lasted through school days and beyond. We took romance seriously and committed early on.

Mountain romance was indeed romance without all the frills of flowers, dining out, road or beach trips, showers of gifts, celebrating sweetest day; maybe a card at Valentine's Day, you get the picture. There was very little money, few automobiles, and very few opportunities for teenagers to work for pay; however,

200

there was always plenty of work on the family farm, but of course this was without any pay. That kind of work never ceased. It was a way of life for small farm mountain folks and as Paul Harvey would say, "Now, the rest of the story".

Will and Doris -- September 1952.

I shall never forget my first date with Doris (my wife of 59 years). It was on a warm and sunny evening at the end of April or the first of May in 1951. I was all of 16 years old. Bill B. and I arranged the date by coupling up with Doris and her friend Agnes. It was strategic planning at its best.

We would ride the bus home with friends; me with Bill and Agnes with Doris to her home. We agreed on meeting at Doris' place later that evening. It was

7:00PM sharp when we arrived. Needless to say, I was extremely anxious as I had never hugged or kissed a girl before, nor had I experienced the attraction I had for Doris or any other girl before. All this stuff stirring in a sixteen year old boy was about all I could take! I don't know what was operating in my friend Bill's stomach or head either. We didn't compare notes nor did we have a plan for the evening. It just took its course.

We met some of Doris' family along with her Mom of course. Her brother, Denver, who I knew from basketball practice (that was comforting) and three more of her siblings were there to greet us. This house full of people all seemed like part of the date.

It didn't take long for the four of us to devise a plan for some alone time together. Young people are so resourceful when it comes time for romance. We decided to walk to a lookout about a half a mile down Doris' road. We walked there and found a grassy spot clear of cow patties (it was a pasture field) and sat there to watch the sunset. Sunsets are one of my favorite things I guess. It was a gorgeous view down through Valley Furnace. The sun was setting, casting long shadows from trees and mountain tops, cattle were grazing in pasture fields as far as we could see, and a few houses had smoke making its way toward heaven and then disappearing. The sun changed from a white ball of fire to a warm orange and then to a red glow as it slowly disappeared over the farthest mountain. Things could not have been choreographed any better for this first date. After the sunset we returned to Doris' house. It was getting dark, it was a weekday, and the occupants were bedding down for the evening. I had calmed down a tad and I think Bill had too. Aah, our time together on the couch; just the four of us, together at last. There we were, the four of us, on the couch in an oil lamp lit living room; it couldn't get any better than this. The usual furniture occupied the room; chairs, a Bible on a side stand, a Burnside stove in the middle of the room (it hadn't been removed for the summer yet – stoves were removed after cold nights were over), a front door on the right, a bedroom door straight ahead and a bedroom door behind us with a kitchen door on the left. It was one of those warm spring evenings, comfortable enough to leave the door open and let the screen door keep out all the night critters such as bugs, fire flies, bats or anything else lurking out there in the dark.

What a set up and wonderful evening for four young people experiencing their first blush with romance. Remember, I had never sat next to (bodies touching) a girl before in my life, but there we were. I was sitting on the left, Doris was next to me, Agnes was next to Doris and then Bill was on the right. I had my right arm on the back of the couch behind Doris and Bill had his left arm behind Agnes, on top of my arm I might add. It was intense with anxiety abound. We sat there for about thirty minutes talking about whatever young people discussed back then. The content of the conversations we had that night was far different than what young people would be discussing today.

It was a bit past 9:00 in the evening and things were still going well; just four kids and romance on the couch. All of a sudden anxiety spilled over the top when Gladys (Doris' Mother) called out from the bedroom behind us in a deep authoritative gravelly voice, "Doris, it's time to go to bed!" Bill and I in concert stood quickly and bolted for the door. I think we took the screen door off the hinges. I certainly hope we didn't. We didn't knock the stove over on our exit either, but I'm not sure if we went through the gate or took out a panel of paling fence on that jettisoned exit. We didn't look back! No hugs, no goodbyes and certainly no kisses. Needless to say, romance ended abruptly at 9:30 on that spring night. I don't remember if we rode or walked back to Bill's house, but in any event the long trip back to his house was therapeutic. What an evening! What an experience! Doris and I have had many good laughs since that first date in May of 1951. See "End of the Road" (Appendix).

You Rang Madam

I grew up in a family that laughed a lot and saw humor in most things, even in tight situations or sobering events. This doesn't mean we responded to burials and losses as if they weren't important; they were and we acted accordingly.

I think we laughed a lot and saw humor due to the mindset that it's easier to laugh than cry and the notion that there's too many poker faced people in the world already. Laughter is such a healthy expression and sometimes a good release from tense moments. My brothers and sister, Betty, were always pulling some prank, joke, or foolishness to get a laugh. They would spend days masterminding a plot and they were good at it. Most set ups were not planned or mean spirited, they just occurred. The point being, we learned to laugh at ourselves and see humor in most things. We still do.

I will give you an example. My wife and I were asleep one night after the usual nightly rituals had been taken care of, such as, close down the house, check door locks (we didn't have to do that in the 1930's to 1960's), visit the necessary room, read a bit (that puts me to sleep), kiss and say goodnight, fall asleep, and snore off and on; you get the picture. Of course you will visit the necessary room occasionally during the night –

that's a given.

On one of those dark, still nights, I was awake, but Doris didn't know it. She stirred and headed towards the necessary room. Halfway there she passed gas; a thunder boomer of sorts. I said in a sober strong voice, "<u>You Rang Madam</u>?" It startled her. She recovered quickly and reprimanded me for my astute comment, entered the necessary room and then she started laughing. We have gotten a few laughs since the "<u>You Rang Madam</u>" event.

Life is tough; look for laughter wherever you can find it. I still believe anything of that magnitude deserved recognition! "<u>You Rang Madam</u>?" is one of my finer astute comments and clever indeed, don't you think?

Family Reunions

As a little kid in the late 1930's, early 1940's, Dad and Mom took us to lots of family reunions. Some of the larger connected families, like the Freemans, Nestors, Ritters, and Moats had an annual event. During this time period I clearly remember the Nestor reunion at Bull Run in Tucker County and the Freeman reunion at Locust Grove Church. At that time, I wasn't all that excited or interested in the program or old folks collecting to swap stories. However, I was interested in the food spread out on mile long tables and the deserts made the sacrifice of attending worthwhile.

The older folks would plan for weeks to prepare food and attend. After the event, they had another week or two of discussion about who was there and those they had not seen in years; who had aged, who looked good, who would not make the next reunion, and who got their feelings hurt.

Now that I have aged a bit I see the importance of reunions and how they help keep families more connected. I have changed from a "food grazer" to a participant and have enjoyed being part of the annual "Ball Reunion" at the Nestorville Community Center over the past twenty plus years. It truly is a time of fun, fellowship and connecting with family. Locals and those who relocated far from Barbour County always enjoy the festivities.

My contributions have been through song, story, and surprises. I will relate one of the surprise events. Brother Hayward has been the M.C., coordinator of events, information distributor and "Ledbetter Jokester" from the beginning. He loves telling the audience new stories about Cletus, Clovis, Chlorine, Uncle Bursey, Nuegene, and so on.

A few years ago at a Ball reunion I related a story about Hayward and my experiences while serving in the Army. Hayward was drafted in May 1953 and I was drafted in September 1953. Our Army paths took very different directions. He wound up in the Honor Guard in Washington, D.C. and I wound up as Company Clerk for the 55 Transportation Battalion Headquarters Company in Korea. While our formal military paths did not cross, activities in our private lives did. I surprised Brother Hayward by telling him at the reunion that I needed to share a secret about both of us meeting and befriending a young woman in central West Virginia during our time in the Army from 1953-1955. Of course it was a different place and time for both of us. He was eager to know who the young lady was. I asked him if he had met a girl from Gassaway, West Virginia sometime during his service years. He pondered the question and reluctantly said yes. I questioned if her name was Beanie. "Yes", he said. I then told him that I had met her as well. The audience was spell bound and wanted more information so of course I complied. I said, "Hayward, we both had the pleasure to meet and spend quality time with Beanie Openport from Gassaway, West Virginia. Beanie was a clerk at the Blowout Gas Company at the time.

I don't know if this revelation caused Brother Hayward any marital discord or not, but when I unwind one of these surprise stories, it disturbs my spouse Doris for days. She wants to know for how long and how in-volved I was with Beanie Openport. It was worth Do-ris' wrath to be able to surprise Hayward and lead the audience down such a primrose path from pages of past history. Some got it while others are probably still working on it.

And What Happened to Moatsville?

(It's no longer on the West Virginia Road Map.)

Within the last five to ten years I discovered that Moatsville was no longer a village on the state road map. I was shocked, stunned, flabbergasted, angry and downright hurt; the place of my birth and growing up years was gone! G-O-N-E. I think removing Moatsville from the state road map is first cousin to identity theft. How dare the map makers in Charleston remove Moatsville? My immediate reaction was to form a "Recovery Committee" and get Moatsville back on the state road map. That committee's first decision, I expect, would be a march and a demonstration to recover the village of Moatsville. And while the committee is at it, why not recover villages like New Moatsville and other small villages in Barbour County that were removed from the map; Sinclair being another one. This recovery movement might just as well go state wide. As Mom would say, "now we're loggin". I already know of one other booster that lives in Clay County. I'm pretty sure he'd join the movement. He lost his town "Corton" to the map makers too. In an article in "Goldenseal", Volume 23, Number 3, fall 1997, it mentions Sinclair in Barbour County and towns in Tucker County, Auviltown, Clover, Hannahsville, and Macedonia as dying villages. Colebank in Preston County no longer has a dot on the West Virginia road map either.

<u>Wake up mountaineers</u>! We're losing our identity and spot on the State Road Map without due process. I don't know about other fellow mountaineers, but I know I want Moatsville back on the map! Current and past Moatsvillians must support the cause and join. There is strength in numbers. Join and let your voices and dollars be heard at the State House. Join today! Send your dollars and coupons to: The Wilberville Foundation. The Foundation will use your contributions for placing Moatsville back on the State Road Map. Honesty regarding your contributions is our motto. Therefore, we are informing you up front that your dollars will be distributed according to the following formula. Ninety eight percent administrative cost for the Wilberville Foundation; one percent for mailing and office supplies; one half percent for telephones with call waiting and a whopping one half of one percent for the map thing. The Foundation desperately needs your contributions to save our town – Moatsville, West Virginia, Zip Code 26405. See "My Allegheny Home" (Appendix).

Appendix

Songs --

The Place I Call Home
Green Apple Quick Step
End of the Road
My Allegheny Home
Right Down the Road
The Moatsville Candy Heist of 1949
Higher Up the Mountain
Walk With the Lord

THE PLACE I CALL HOME

Will Ball – Wilberville Publications (July 2004)

OH MY WEST VIRGINIA, A GREAT PLACE TO WORK, PLAY AND ROAM, THE HILLS, THE HILLS OF WEST VIRGINIA, IS THE PLACE I'LL ALWAYS CALL HOME.

FROM HARPERS FERRY TO SPRUCE KNOB, YOU'LL FIND THE LOW AND HIGH, ELKINS DOWN TO PRINCETON, THE WEATHER CHANGES AS YOU PASS BY.

FROM THE POTOMAC – TO THE OHIO, THERE'S RIVERS EVERYWHERE, IF YOU RAFT THE GAULEY OR THE NEW, THEY'LL REMEMBER YOU WERE THERE.

FROM BLUEFIELD TO PARKERSBURG, THERE'S A SCENIC HIGHWAY, HUNTINGTON TO THE SULPHER SPRINGS, ROUTE 64 WILL TAKE YOU ALL THE WAY.

CHORUS (AGAIN)

THERE'S HARNESS RACES AT CHARLESTOWN, SKIING CANAAN OR OLD SNOWSHOE, DRAG RACES EVERYWHERE, THERE'S ALWAYS SOMETHING TO DO.

THERE'S ENTERTAINMENT AT THE WHEELING JAMBOREE, AND AT EVERY WATERING HOLE, CHURCHES UP AND DOWN THE HILL SIDE, TO SAVE YOUR PRECIOUS SOUL.

FROM THE GRAND BALLROOM AT THE GREENBRIAR, TO THE LOWLIEST LITTLE SHACK, KIN FOLKS IN WEST VIRGINIA, WILL ALWAYS HAVE YOUR BACK.

PRETTY GIRLS IN THE MOUNTAINS, PRETTY ONES
IN THE DELL,
MOUNTAIN BOYS WILL FIND THE ONE, THAT
REALLY RINGS THEIR BELL.

CHORUS (AGAIN)

THERE'S STEEL MILLS IN WEIRTON, AND COAL
MINES ALONG THE TUG,
CHEMICAL PLANTS AROUND CHARLESTON, AND
CONSTRUCTION WORKERS IN THE MUD.

PEOPLE WORK THE COAL MINES, AND ON TRAINS
THAT HAUL IT AWAY,
THEY TAKE GAS AND OIL FROM UNDER THE DIRT,
THAT'S HOW THEY EARN THEIR PAY.

THEY HAVE PEACHES IN THE SUMMER TIME, APPLES
IN THE FALL,
GARDNERS THROUGHOUT THE STATE, THEY CAN
GROW IT ALL.

A LITTLE BIT OF EVERYTHING, TAKEN FROM THE
LAND,
KEEPS MOUNTAINEERS INDEPENDENT, AND TAKES
CARE OF THEIR CLAN.

215

Green Apple Quick Step

Will Ball – November 2008 (Wilberville Publications)

My Daddy was a quiet man, few words did he say;
Only time he'd open up, was when he found his way;
To that green apple cider keg, down at Annon's mill.

He would visit often, and they would set a spell;
Talk about their crops and things, and no water in the well;
Drinkin' green apple cider, down at Annon's mill.

They would hug that cider keg, many times before the night was through;
Stick a straw in the bung hole, and have a snort or two,
Of that green apple cider, down at Annon's Mill.

Then he would loosen up, and even try to sing;
Around that old cider keg, when he felt the sting;
Of that green apple cider, down at Annon's Mill.

When he stood – to go home, he'd have a swimming head;
And do the green apple quick step, not knowing where it led;
He'd do the green apple quick step, not knowing where it led.

He'd do the green apple quick step, all the way home;
Two steps up, one step back, swearing never more to roam;
Or drink that green apple cider, down at Annon's mill.
Drink that green apple cider, at Annon's mill.

216

END OF THE ROAD

(JULY 2008 – JANUARY 2009)

WILL BALL – (WILBERVILLE PUBLICATIONS)

I WAS DRIVING DOWN A COUNTRY HIGHWAY, MY
MIND WAS TAKING ME BACK IN TIME,
BACK TO A GIRL AT THE END OF THE ROAD, AND NOT
KNOWING IF SHE'D BE MINE.

WHEN WE MET ON HER OLD ROAD, WE'D WALK TO THE
OTHER END,
WALK AND TALK ABOUT WHAT LAY AHEAD, GOING
PLACES I'D NEVER BEEN.

THEN TEARS STARTED ROLLING DOWN MY FACE, FROM
PLACES I DIDN'T UNDERSTAND,
'TIL PAGES OF MEMORY RAN THROUGH MY MIND, OF
PLACES I'D ALREADY BEEN.

TODAY IT SEEMS A SHORT, SHORT TIME, SINCE WE LEFT
THAT OLD ROAD,
SHE TO THE CITY AND I OFF TO WAR, NOT KNOWING IF
WE'D EVER MEET AGAIN.

THEN WE MET AGAIN AFTER LEAVING THAT OLD
ROAD, AND WE'VE BEEN TOGETHER SINCE THEN,
HAD OUR SHARE OF SUNSHINE AND RAIN, GOING
PLACES WE'D NEVER BEEN.

OH YES, IT'S BEEN A LONG, LONG TIME,
AND THERE'S WHERE IT ALL BEGAN,
AND IF I HAD MY LIFE TO LIVE OVER, I'D
DO IT ALL OVER AGAIN.

I'D DO IT ALL OVER AGAIN.

MY ALLEGHENY HOME

Will Ball – Wilberville Publications (December 2007)

I CAN HEAR THOSE ALLEGHENY MOUNTAINS
    CALLING, CALLING ME BACK TO MY HOME;
BACK TO MEMORIES OF FRIENDS AND FAMILY,
    AND TO PLACES WHERE I USED TO ROAM.

AS A YOUNG MAN DETERMINED TO WANDER,
    HAD TO KNOW WHAT'S AROUND THE BEND;
DIDN'T KNOW WHAT I WAS LEAVING, TIL I WAS
    A THOUSAND MILES FROM MY HOME.

TOOK A MILLION MILES AND THIRTY YEARS OF WANDERING,
    TO KNOW WHO I WAS AND WHERE I BELONGED;
NOW I'M ON MY WAY BACK TO FRIENDS AND FAMILY,
    GOING BACK TO MY ALLEGHENY HOME.

THEY'LL BE WAITING FOR ME WHEN I GET THERE,
    AND I KNOW THAT SOME ARE ALREADY GONE;
SPEND TIME WITH MOM AND DAD ON THE HILLSIDE,
    WHEN I GET BACK TO MY ALLEGHENY HOME.

CALLING ME, CALLING ME – CALLING ME BACK
TO MY ALLEGHENY HOME.

RIGHT DOWN THE ROAD

Will Ball – Wilberville Publications (August 2007)

THERE'S A LITTLE BIT OF HEAVEN RIGHT
DOWN THE ROAD,
SWEET AS A ROSE BUD AND EVERYBODY KNOWS,
THAT SHE WON'T WAIT FOREVER, WHEN SHE'S
GOT LOVIN ON HER MIND,
SHE'LL BE GONE WITH SOME YOUNG MAN,
COME THE END OF HARVEST TIME.

I HOPE I'M THAT LUCKY MAN, WHEN ALL IS
SAID AND DONE;
I KNOW THAT SHE'S THE ONLY ONE THAT I'VE
BEEN THINKING OF.
BUT DADDY SAID "NOW LISTEN SON, AND LET'S
GET ONE THING CLEAR;
SHE'S TOO YOUNG AND SO ARE YOU, YOU'LL
WAIT ANOTHER YEAR".

BUT THERE'S JOHN AND JAKE AND POSSUM
TATE, WALKING UP AND DOWN OUR ROAD;
AND OTHER YOUNG MEN HANGING AROUND,
WAITING TO CALL.
I KNOW THAT I CAN'T WAIT THAT LONG, OR
SHE'LL BE GONE FOR SURE,
I KNOW WHAT MY DADDY SAID, BUT I CAN'T
WAIT ANOTHER YEAR.

WHEN I WENT THERE TO SEE HER, LATER ON
THAT FALL;
HER DADDY SAID, "NOW SON SHE'S NOT HERE,
SHE WENT AWAY WITH THE LAST YOUNG
MAN THAT CAME TO CALL".
THEY'VE GONE AWAY I THINK THEY'LL STAY,
SOMEWHERE UP THE LINE,
SHE SAID TO GIVE HER LOVE TO YOU, AND
SHE'LL BE BACK NEXT HARVEST TIME".

THE MOATSVILLE CANDY HEIST OF 1949

Will Ball – Wilberville Publications (December 2000)

I'M SURPRISED WE'RE NOT ALL STILL DOING TIME,
FOR THAT CANDY TRUCK ROBBERY IN 1949,
UP TETER CREEK ROAD IN MOATSVILLE, WEST VIRGINIA.
THEY WERE BOTH GOOD FRIENDS OF MINE, WE'VE
REGRETTED THAT NIGHT MANY A TIME,
THE MOATSVILLE CANDY HEIST OF 1949.

WHEN THAT DELIVERY TRUCK LEFT NEVE GALLS'
STORE, WE WAITED PATIENTLY UPON THAT FOREST FLOOR,
IT WAS THERE WE PLANNED TO OUTRUN THAT
TRUCK, AND THEN CLIMB ON BOARD;
WE CAUGHT THAT TRUCK FROM BEHIND, BILLY
CLIMBED ON BOARD AND WILLARD AND I FELL IN LINE;
AS BILLY HANDED BOX AFTER BOX OF CANDY OUT
THE DOOR, THE MOATSVILLE CANDY HEIST OF 1949.

WE HAD ALL OUR ARMS COULD HOLD, WE
THOUGHT WE HAD JUST STRUCK GOLD,
WHEN BILLY JUMPED OFF THAT TRUCK AND WE
WATCHED AS IT ROLLED OUT OF SIGHT,
ON THAT HISTORICAL NIGHT IN 1949.

THE SPOILS OF THAT HEIST WE DID DIVIDE, EQUAL
SHARES WE HELD WITH PRIDE, RIGHT THERE ON
THAT ROAD IN 1949,
BUT ALL THAT JOY CAME CRASHING DOWN, WHEN
WE REACHED THE EDGE OF TOWN,
CARRYING OUR STASH FROM THE HEIST OF 1949.

AS WE STOOD THERE ON THAT NIGHT, A CONSCIOUS
THOUGHT CAME INTO SIGHT,
AND BELIEVE ME IT WAS A SOBERING THOUGHT,

ABOUT ALL THAT STUFF THAT WE HAD NOT BOUGHT;
AND HOW ARE WE GOING TO EXPLAIN THIS TO OUR
MOMS AND DADS, GONNA GET THE LIVING HELL
BEAT OUT OF US, FOR THE CANDY HEIST OF 1949.

WHAT A LESSON WE DID LEARN, ON THAT NIGHT
OF OUR SOJOURN,
THE CANDY HEIST OF 1949, FORGIVE US LORD FOR
THE MOATSVILLE CANDY HEIST OF 1949.

Higher up the Mountain

Will Ball – Wilberville Publications - July 2006

WHEN I WAS JUST A BOY MY MOMMA TOLD ME,
GO HIGHER UP THE MOUNTAIN BOY, THAT'S WERE
YOU OUGHT TO BE;
WHERE YOU OUGHT TO BE BOY – IT'S WHERE YOU
OUGHT TO BE,
HIGHER UP THE MOUNTAIN – IT'S WHERE YOU
OUGHT TO BE.

THOUGHT I'D TRY THE CITY LIFE, I FOUND IT NOT FOR ME,
THEN I HEARD MOMMA'S WORDS AGAIN –
MOUNTAINS IS WHERE YOU'LL BE;
MOUNTAINS IS WHERE YOU'LL BE BOY, MOUNTAINS
IS WHERE YOU'LL BE,
I TRIED THE CITY LIFE AND FOUND IT NOT FOR ME.

SUN COMES UP ON THE MOUNTAIN TOP BEFORE
IT'S UP DOWN BELOW,
WHEN EVENING COMES THE SUN'S STILL ON THE
MOUNTAIN TOP AND LONG GONE DOWN BELOW;
LONG GONE DOWN BELOW BOYS – LONG GONE BELOW,
SUN'S STILL ON THE MOUNTAIN TOP AND LONG
GONE DOWN BELOW.

SOME FOLKS LIVE IN THE VALLEY – SOME UPON THE HILL,
OTHERS UP THE MOUNTAIN WITH THE
WHIPPOORWILL;
WITH THE WHIPPOORWILL BOYS, WITH
WHIPPOORWILL,
HIGHER UP THE MOUNTAIN WITH THE
WHIPPOORWILL.

IF GIRLS ARE PRETTIER UP THE MOUNTAIN, RECKON
WHERE I'LL BE,
HIGH ON YONDER MOUNTAIN FOR ALL THE GIRLS

TO SEE;
FOR ALL THE GIRLS TO SEE BOYS – FOR ALL THE
GIRLS TO SEE,
HIGH ON YONDER MOUNTAIN FOR ALL THE GIRLS
TO SEE.

SHE LIVED UP THE MOUNTAIN, I LIVED DOWN BELOW,
FURTHER UP THE MOUNTAIN IS WHERE I WANT TO GO;
WHERE I WANT TO GO BOYS, IT'S WHERE I WANT TO GO,
FURTHER UP THE MOUNTAIN IS WHERE I WANT TO GO.

NOW WE'RE ON THE MOUNTAIN TOP, MY TRUE LOVE
AND ME,
LIVING ON THE MOUNTAIN TOP CAUSE SHE
MARRIED ME;
TRUE LOVE MARRIED ME BOYS – TRUE LOVE MARRIED ME,
LIVING ON THE MOUNTAIN TOP, CAUSE SHE MARRIED ME.

RECKON HIGHER UP THE MOUNTAIN IS WHERE I'LL STAY,
HIGHER UP THE MOUNTAIN, WON'T YOU COME
ALONG TODAY;
COME ALONG TODAY BOYS – COME ALONG TODAY,
RECKON HIGHER UP THE MOUNTAIN IS WHERE I'M
GONNA STAY.

WHEN THE DAY IS OVER AND THE SUN IS SINKING LOW,
WE'LL BE ON THE PORCH WHEN THE SUN GOES
DOWN BELOW;
WHEN THE SUN GOES DOWN BELOW BOYS – WHEN
THE SUN GOES DOWN BELOW,
SITTING ON THE PORCH WHEN THE SUN GOES
DOWN BELOW.

NOW WHEN I'M OLD AND GRAY, TELL YOU WHERE I'LL BE,
HIGH ON YONDER MOUNTAIN UNDER THAT OLD
PINE TREE;
UNDER THAT OLD PINE TREE BOYS – UNDER THAT
OLD PINE TREE,
SIX FEET UNDER THE CLAY BOYS, 'NEATH THAT OLD
PINE TREE.

WALK WITH THE LORD

Will Ball – Wilberville Publications (March 2005)

WOKE UP AT THREE THIS MORNING WITH A
SONG IN MY HEAD,
SAT UP AND LISTENED TO THE WORDS AND
HERE'S WHAT THEY SAID;

WON'T YOU WALK WITH THE LORD, OH WON'T
YOU WALK WITH THE LORD,
HE'S THE KING OF ZION AND STANDS ON HIS
WORD;
HE'LL HOLD YOU CLOSE TO HIS BOSOM AND
KEEP YOU SAFE FROM ALL HARM,
WALK WITH JESUS AND PRAISE HIS HOLY
NAME.

OH, YES WE'LL WALK WITH THE LORD, WE'RE
GONNA WALK WITH THE LORD,
GONNA WALK WITH THE SAVIOR AND PRAISE
HIS HOLY NAME.

WE'LL SEE JOHN THE BAPTIST, DANIEL AND
MARY TOO,
WON'T BE MANY SINNERS THERE TO HELP
PULL US THROUGH;
WE'LL SEE PAUL AND SILAS, ST. PETER AT THE
PEARLY GATES,
WALK WITH THE SAVIOR AND HE WON'T HAVE
YOU WAIT.

NOW WHEN YOU'RE TIRED AND WEARY, HAVE
TROUBLED DAYS TO GET THROUGH,
GIVE IT TO THE SAVIOR, 'CAUSE HE'S GONNA
GET US THROUGH;

WE'LL SEE MOSES AND THE PROMISE LAND,
WON'T NEED A ROAD MAP IN OUR HAND,
WE'RE GONNA WALK THE PROMISE LAND,
'CAUSE HE'S GONNA WALK US THROUGH.

Postscript

Now that you have read this Book, you most likely realize that God has been "<u>undercover</u>" with me all my life. I hope He has been there for you as well.

I am also hopeful that you enjoyed the journey with me as we visited events, people and places that have not changed in my memory vault.

Cheers.